The Depression Optimist

21 Must Ask Questions and Answers About Depression

Andrew Richardson

Copyright © 2014 Andrew Richardson

All rights reserved.

ISBN: 1500788708
ISBN-13: 978-1500788704

DEDICATION

To Lily and Isabella

We give depression too much respect. That it can be so devastating blinds us to the truth that it is typically straightforward to understand and to recover. This book is aiming in a small way to correct this awful imbalance – on behalf of all the many millions who are so short changed by the conventional depression "wisdom".

In doing so I am inspired by my teachers – notably Joe Griffin and Ivan Tyrell (the founders of the Human Givens) and by so many of my clients, who by their openness and humanity have convinced me that when it comes to Depression recovery, I know what I am about.

CONTENTS

ACKNOWLEDGMENTS 1

PART ONE: 21 MUST ASK QUESTIONS AND ANSWERS ABOUT DEPRESSION 2

1. How to get help with depression? 3

2. What are the causes of depression? 6

3. What are the symptoms of depression? 8

4. What are the options for depression treatment? 10

5. What are the signs of depression? 15

6. How to cure depression? 17

7. What is the recommended counselling option for depression? 20

8. The best way on how to treat depression? 23

9. What are the signs of depression in women? 26

10. What are the signs of depression in men? 29

11. Depression UK - what is depression? 31

12. Who can I trust to help me with my Depression? 34

13. Why is just talking about your problems never enough on its own? ... 36

14. Why is the NHS so unsatisfactory for depression? 38

15. Why do people get depressed? 41

16. Why are anti-depressants not the answer for me? 44

17. Why is most counselling, including Cognitive Behavioural Therapy, such hard work? 46

18. Is Depression an illness that needs me to trust my GP and the NHS? 48

19. I seem to have been depressed for most of my life – it must surely be an illness? 50

20. Want to know the three steps to depression recovery? 53

21. What's the best depression help I can get? 56

PART 2: ARTICLES FROM THE DEPRESSION OPTIMIST 59

CHAPTER 22: GOOD THERAPY – HOW COUNSELLING WORKS 60

CHAPTER 23: AN INTRODUCTION TO HUMAN GIVENS 79

CHAPTER 24: HOME TRUTHS ABOUT DEPRESSION HELP ON THE NHS 99

CHAPTER 25 MY CLIENT'S EXPERIENCES OF DEPRESSION RECOVERY 115
CHAPTER 26: BE A DEPRESSION RECOVERY OPTIMIST 141
ABOUT THE AUTHOR 156

ACKNOWLEDGMENTS

What are my credentials and authority – for speaking so hopefully on depressor and so critically of the depression help industry

I am simply a private practitioner trained in the Human Givens approach who over the past eight years has helped many scores of my clients recover quickly from their depression. I have seen at first hand how short changed many have been by the NHS and the failures of both antidepressants and CBT to help them. While on the other hand I have been able to test and adapt what Human Givens teaches are the causes of most depressions and how to relieve them quickly. So I know that these ideas are broadly right and will apply to most sufferers of depression.

And it is this conviction that is my motivation – to explain what a depression is and how to relieve it, the stories of some of my patients, on what Human Givens is about, what I believe makes good counselling and going all the way up to very critical commentary on the depression help industry and those who do so little good and at times considerable harm.

Andrew Richardson

PART ONE

21 MUST ASK QUESTIONS AND ANSWERS ABOUT DEPRESSION

1. How to get help with depression?

It may seem a strange thing to say but given the overwhelming ignorance of what a depression is, it is important that right at the beginning you have a basic understanding of what your depression is about. And the fact that you may be lost in a depression right now does not mean that you cannot understand what a depression is as well as anybody else – and maybe better. So what is a depression is all about? Well, this is it – and as you read, my guess is that it will seem obvious to you.

Depression is mental and emotional exhaustion – no more no less. And that the exhaustion is so great and leaves you so helpless that it fuels terror and despair – which of course simply adds to the pressure.

It follows therefore that you need to look for help from anyone who can take pressure off you as this will allow you to begin to take the steps necessary to get your life working again.

You need to speak to people who are sympathetic to the idea that you are doing your best but something is just not allowing you to help yourself. And you want to keep well away from anybody who thinks that you are ill and that there is something profoundly wrong with you and that you need to get lost in a medical approach, with medical treatment and diagnosis and medication and pseudo science and all of that.

Think of depression like a twisted ankle. Yes it can

hurt like hell and stop you walking and doing all kinds of things. But you are not ill in the accepted sense and indeed all you need to do if you have twisted your ankle is to rest it. And so with most depressions, you absolutely must rest your mind.

Imagine that you were crushed under a rock in an earthquake. And you were screaming and panicking and your legs were broken and useless. No-one would say you were mad or delusional to be screaming, even though it may not be doing you any good.

And again I will say it - so it is with depression

You need to seek help from people who understand that depression is the end point of a vicious circle that has been feeding on itself and making things worse and worse - to the dead end where you find yourself now. And that they understand that healing comes from reversing this into a virtuous circle where change leads to more change and improvement and so on.

Ask those from whom you are seeking help what they understand a depression is. And listen carefully to the reply. Is the answer hidden behind medical jargon and spurious diagnosis and a focus on symptoms, such as low mood which of course means nothing? You should also be very suspicious if the first port of call is to suggest anti-depressants.

I'm not saying there are no circumstances where anti-depressants might not be of assistance for a temporary period BUT that they will almost never be the main and exclusive way. And whether they do help or not is a matter of luck. It's a scattergun. In other words, antidepressants might work but then again they might make things a whole lot worse.

And finally, be very suspicious of those who think that your depression will be helped by you immediately talking about your problems and letting you unload. Now this may well be something that you also think you need as your head is exploding with questions and worries and theories. But to unload like this when you are exhausted will at best give you short term relief .... and perhaps not even that. Either way the result will basically be to keep you stuck and exhausted and staying lost in exhausting and useless rumination.

2. What are the causes of depression?

When understanding the causes of depression you have to distinguish between the immediate causes and the longer term causes. In terms of the immediate causes it is very simple. A depression is the exhaustion caused by ruminating and worrying too much and this is so damaging because it means that you have to dream more than your exhausted brain can cope with – as you attempt unsuccessfully to clear your head.

Rumination, leading to exhausting over dreaming and so further rumination but critically, no meaningful action. This is what causes your brain to become exhausted and to overload.

We dream every night and what we are doing when we dream is essential mind maintenance. Like an emotional flush toilet, we are getting rid of the previous day's uncompleted worries, anxieties, and angers and so on – in order to be ready for the next day. But dreaming takes a lot of energy so if we have to dream a lot (because we have lived that day full up with unproductive worrying and fears), then that will exhaust us. And then our ability to deal with our problems unravels further, creating more worrying and rumination and exhaustion

If you understand why you dream, then you understand depression

Many describe depression as being locked in their worrying brain, unable to escape from useless and obsessive rumination, often of a "what is wrong with me" nature - a terrifying trance state of inward obsession. To be depressed is an added layer of misery often piled upon genuine challenges, further reducing the person's ability to cope with their difficulties

And what feeds the depression – the fundamental causes if you like? There are three.

First, these will relate to the difficulty of your life situation now and the nature and extent of the crisis that might have triggered your depression?

Then second, there are your resources and capacities. How well are your emotions, habitual patterns of thinking and responding helping or not helping to get your life working as you need it to?

Third and finally, it is important to discover if there is trauma lurking somewhere in your past as often it is the active reliving of past traumas that is the main inhibitor to one's capacity to get a life that is working better for you.

3. What are the symptoms of depression?

For depressed people, the mornings are the worst time of day. That's it in a nutshell – the most reliable symptom of a depression.

And if you have read the previous chapter (chapter 2) – about the role of dreaming you will know why the mornings are so bad.

I described the role of dreaming as essential mind maintenance – designed to clear our mind for the next day. Like an emotional flush toilet. But I said also that dreaming takes a lot of energy. And so if you have to dream a lot because you spent a lot of time during the previous day worrying and ruminating without getting anywhere – then the next morning when your body can dream no more, you will typically wake feeling terrible – tired without energy or motivation. Does that make sense?

It's that simple and straightforward. The day is then likely to improve, though not always by very much.

Now compare that with the typical list of depression symptoms you will find pretty well wherever else you look. These lists are all much the same. And you will see that each and every one of the symptoms on the typical list follows from the exhaustion of worrying too much and waking up tired.

Here is that typical list:

- Feeling miserable and sad, being exhausted, finding the smallest tasks impossible
- Losing any sense of enjoyment
- Feeling a failure, guilty and a burden and that life is not worth living or passing you by
- Being tense and irritable all the time
- Avoiding people, losing self confidence

You can see that having no self confidence, getting no meaning and pleasure and preferring to hide away are all of a piece with exhausting over worrying. You can also see that this list of depression symptoms have one thing in common. It is that they all omit the most important symptom – which is the exhaustion when you wake up in the morning. And that all the symptoms on the list follow from that.

There is a final symptom which is to be found on a number of depression symptom lists. This is aches and pains which appear to have no physical cause. But you are never told that this follows from the lack of healthy deep wave regenerating sleep which has been squeezed by the overwhelming need to dream and REM sleep. That this will tend to lead to these physical problems which of course adds to unproductive worrying.

Is the early morning the worst time of the day for you?

4. What are the options for depression treatment?

Well how long is a piece of string? There are as many ideas about lifting depression as there are days in the year and probably more than that. And many of them make a lot of sense as far as they go.

So, who could argue with advice that says you should take exercise and eat well? And it is self evidently good for us to connect to and to be busy engaging in activities that take us out of ourselves. And so many sources and books will focus on this. I remember reading a blog about how poetry had helped a woman overcome her depression. So there you go – not that I would rely on that one.

But what all of these tips (that's all I would call them) lack is an overriding idea of what depression is and where all of these tips fit in.

So while I recognise a lot of what is being said as being very worthwhile and for sure, if you investigate self help books and read websites or go to people who seem to be inspiring you, then it is unlikely that any of what you learn will do you any harm and it may in fact help a bit. But if you really are lost in the depths of depression and truly exhausted with your head going round and round - it is unlikely that much of these tips will do much good either.

Beyond this potpourri of self help and good ideas, I would say there are three options for depression treatment. The first is to go to your GP and take the antidepressants that will almost certainly be on offer. The second is to wait for cognitive behavioural therapy or

CBT, again through your GP. But I'm afraid neither antidepressants nor CBT is really the answer.

Briefly, antidepressants can help to change moods and take some pressure off - but no one knows ahead of time whether you will be one of the lucky ones or one of those unlucky individuals who become addicted, suffer side effects (including suicidal thoughts) and will either get no benefit at all or feel worse. The problem is that antidepressants do not directly deal with the main cause of depression which is useless rumination and dreaming too much that feeds a life that is not working. And though this is not the time to critique all of the so called evidence in support of antidepressants as a worthwhile depression treatment – just take my word for it that the evidence ain't what its cracked up to be. For example, a recent review of the evidence by a Danish researcher (Prof Gotzsche) concluded that *"evidence for the benefits of psychiatric drugs, like antidepressants, was so weak and flawed – and adverse effects so often under-rated or ignored – that the widespread use of these drugs was likely to be doing more harm than good".*

And how about this from a survey of 1829 New Zealanders who had been prescribed antidepressants?

"Although 82% reported the drugs had helped alleviate their depression, over a third reported suicidal feelings that they attributed to the drug and this rose to more than half of those aged between 18 to 25. Nearly 2/3 reported suffering from sexual difficulties and other effects including feeling emotionally numb (60%) feeling not like myself (50%) reduction in positive feelings (40%) and withdrawal effects (55%).

This is what the lead researcher Prof Reid had to say:

"The medicalisation of sadness and distress has received bizarre levels. One in 10 people in some countries are now prescribed antidepressants each year. While the biological side effects of antidepressants such as weight gain and nausea are well documented the psychological interpersonal effects had been largely ignored in tonight. They appear to be alarmingly common."

Neither does CBT (cognitive bahavioural therapy) get to the heart of it. CBT is designed to challenge thoughts and to stop them in their tracks. It is hard work and if you're exhausted to begin with, it will simply be too much. But it's worse than that for if the emotions of exhaustion and fear and collapsing self confidence are driving the thought – then how can CBT be any better than say trying to mow lawn with a pair of scissors or emptying a bath full of water with a teaspoon?

Let me quote Amanda who wrote to me about her experience with CBT.

I did cognitive behavioural therapy. It had limited success as it worked for awhile, however I found myself so tense all the time from having to evaluate every single thought I had 24 hours a day every day. Eventually my defences would wear down and I would relax and then I would slip right back into depression again. It was defeating and killed my hope. The CBT therapists never understood that once those strong feeling took over I was done for and my ability to think clearly rationally disappeared. CBT couldn't help me then.

I think that Amanda's is part of the explanation for the results of a recent evaluation of the NHS's grandly entitled IAPT programme. IAPT stands for Improving

Access to Psychological Therapies, is almost entirely built around CBT and is the NHS's alternative to complete dependence on antidepressants as a depression treatment. What the evidence shows is that IAPT is doing precisely the opposite. It seems that just 10% of participants are getting any benefit at all (Therapy Today 2013).

Before leaving the NHS is worth spending a little while talking about mindfulness or meditation practice as this has now become very fashionable – based on academic evidence that it can help with depression. You might even be offered mindfulness meditation on the NHS. But again, if you are exhausted and dreaming far too much you just don't have the resources to meditate and be mindful. And so though both are very good for many people and I have on occasion recommended it, they only become really helpful and really useful when a lot of progress has been made beforehand – to reduce your mental and emotional exhaustion.

Which brings us on to the third option – namely conventional counselling or talking therapy. The idea is that the going through of the problems with someone who has experience will help – that there will be a breakthrough or insight or clarity that will help. I wish. Without intending to denigrate what I'm sure are many excellent therapists, who can and do help, it is important to understand that talking about your problems is rarely the answer if indeed you begin in a state of exhaustion with emotions way out of control.

The bottom line is that notwithstanding the existence of many good and capable therapists the system and the ideas that animate the system are not helpful for those suffering from depression. If indeed I am right -- that depression is exhaustion and rumination in response to a life that isn't working that is simply unraveling out of control.

5. What are the signs of depression?

First let me remind you of what a depression is?

A depression is an utter exhaustion of the mind – where worries multiply and cannot be controlled or relieved and where rest and relief appear impossible, however hard you try. And by God you are trying. And the apparent impossibility of any rest and recovery fuels the worry and so exhaustion multiplies until for some it can appear unendurable.

And if you remember from previous chapters, the exhaustion causes far too much high energy and exhausting dreaming which feeds the despair. I have talked of the early mornings when you awaken as the very worst time of the day. Does that make sense to you?

Another way to comprehend this is to get a sense of how this awful state of affairs is experienced by those lost in depression. The exhaustion is fed by a mind out of control that, however hard you try and whatever you tell yourself you just cannot stop worrying and ruminating and coming to all kinds of awful conclusions about how pathetic, useless, guilty and shameful you are. And this is how people talk about it - all of these descriptions come from clients of mine, before they recovered of course.

- *Locked in a burning room, with the impossibility of escape and the flames just get closer.*

- *Of being bound securely on a treadmill that cannot be*

stopped so that all you can do is to keep running despite utter exhaustion.

- *Of becoming obsessed with the idea of suicide as the one certain means of escape and this is so terrifying.*

- *Of a fearful terror borne of complete helplessness that then fuels anger or a desperate isolation borne of shame and then indeed the full gamut of overwhelming and drowning emotions.*

- *Of being a car that is flooded with petrol – so you just stop with a judder.*

- *And at times an ice cold clarity of thought – however fleeting and beguiling*

And finally, let me quote from a recent client who explained it beautifully. This is what she said:

- *I can't control my emotions or keep them where they can help me. I feel saturated in them, exhausted and no other part of me is getting a look in. So I just cannot help myself.*

Waking exhausted in the morning, worrying too much, collapsing self confidence and the terror of a mind out of control and there is no escape.

Those are the signs of depression

6. How to cure depression?

This in summary is my three stage programme to cure depression.

The first stage is to build Hope where currently there is none. To begin to see that there is light at the end of the tunnel.

The second is what I call Firefighting - which means doing whatever it takes to get worrying down, rumination under some degree of control even if apparently temporarily - so that sleep improves, you dream less and begin to feel less exhausted.

And then the third step is a Partnership - between you and me to sort out the problems that probably push or pushed you into depression.

Let me go into a little bit of detail on each.

Hope is essential even if in the beginning it's just a small flicker because the absence of hope is the sad experience of so many who are depressed and just cannot see a way out however hard they try (and of course they are trying far too hard). And to build hope for many is to understand what a depression is, to understand the approach that I use – based on the Human Givens and the critical role of dreaming and worrying too much and the vicious circle that it creates.

When building hope and to give a sense that my clients are not going mad I use a metaphor of a twisted ankle.

Yes a twisted ankle can hurt like hell and swell up and look awful but it's not illness in the normal sense of that word and that there is a knowingness by us all that what we have to do is to rest the ankle and then it will heal. And so a depression is like a twisted ankle. You must rest your mind and let it heal. The last thing you would do with a twisted ankle would be to go running and walking on it in the panicky belief that if you didn't you might never walk again - and so ignoring that what you actually need to do is to rest the ankle. Similarly what you need to do with depression is to rest your mind.

In the next fire fighting stage, you need to do whatever it takes to worry a little less. Distraction by physical exercise, by doing things differently and by filling up your time however hard it seems. So you worry a little less and so dream a little less also. And then you will wake up a little bit more refreshed and begin a virtuous circle. For my depressed clients, this is an amazing experience – to prove to themselves by their own direct experience that this depression explanation – of worry, leading to over dreaming, leading to exhaustion is right for them.

Imagine having a simple explanation of why you are feeling as you are feeling, and then beginning to test it and prove it to yourself by a direct experience of feeling better? Wow - how empowering is that?!

The third stage is to work in partnership , to get your life working better and to sort out the issues and the emotional patterns that are clearly stopping you. Having your life working better is the biggest step of all for some clients, while for others - well they can do much of it themselves because they are feeling calmer and more in control.

In considering what our partnership might require, we are going to the heart of what good therapy should be about. And speaking as therapist with a proven track record, I have learnt to rely very much on what the Human Givens approach has taught me – and then to trust my intuition as to how I adapt and use the Human Given's ideas in the circumstances that I find with each of my clients.

First of all I will be looking to see if there are trauma memories that we need to clear before we go any further. And like all Human Givens therapists I have the trance tools to do this. Second, I will be looking to see what your strengths and resources are - and how we can use these to get you taking the steps that move you in the direction that you need to move. A large part of the work that is needed may be about reframing. What this means is to help you to change your perspective to how you see things and how you react - in order to give you control and confidence.

It's a big topic and there is more on this in chapters 22 and 23. But without doubt sustainable change is more than possible especially if stage one (building hope) and stage two (fire fighting to reduce arousal and improve sleep) have prepared the ground.

7. What is the recommended counselling option for depression?

There is no doubt that in the public domain, this is cognitive behavioural therapy (CBT) which currently carries all before it. It is the therapy of choice in the NHS and consequently there is now a burgeoning CBT industry. You will find CBT in the insurance industry and often the first port of call for private individuals. There are prestigious institutions and university departments devoted to CBT research and so there are livelihoods to be made and jobs is to be protected. And why is this you may ask? Is there unequivocal evidence that CBT is superior to the alternatives? No is the answer. In fact on the contrary, there is overwhelming evidence that no single model of therapy is better than any other. I know, amazing to think that but believe me it's true. What CBT is, is no worse than any of the others and it appears to be relatively quick and therefore cheap. And that is why the NHS has been infiltrated by CBT and has now been taken over.

I just talked about the evidence that shows quite conclusively that CBT is no better than any other therapy model. In fact it goes much further than this. It is hard to believe but it is true - that there is no evidence that any therapy model is ever any better than any other. Which is a staggering conclusion and it flies in the face of everything that we intuitively believe. Afterall we believe in hierarchy don't we?. Some models must be better than the others such that there are some cars that are better than others and some football teams are better than others and that the only question is to find the best. That is not though how counselling works. Every therapy model is as good as each other. This is the dodo bird verdict which is based on the Lewis Carroll story in which everybody runs the race and everybody wins and so all must have prizes.

There is though another very powerful conclusion from the evidence of what works best in therapy - from many different therapies in many different circumstances and all over the world. It is even more surprising and it is this. That though no model of therapy has ever been shown to be better than any other, some therapists are better than others. So it's not the model of therapy that counts, it is the therapist and whatever the therapist says she does in her consulting room is really not very important. Much more important than the model of therapy that she purports to follow is that you choose a good therapist.

Now if you were to evaluate CBT and compare it to a whole range of more traditional talking counselling models such as person centred or integrative and the like and going all the way to the other extreme of Freudian analytical long-term therapy -- my sympathies would be more with CBT. Though it is about challenging thoughts rather than feelings which are much more important, CBT does at least have a future focus and it can help quite quickly. Traditional talking therapy of the "tell me how you feel" type is altogether less appealing to me while Freudian therapy which can take years and get you absolutely nowhere is to my mind a close to scandalous and fraudulent approach.

And so if you are looking to find a good therapist and

you are less concerned about the model, these are the questions I would ask.

- Do they convey confidence that they know what they're doing and that they believe in what they are doing?
- Are they flexible and if something is not working will they try something else?
- Do they ask for feedback from you about what is working and what is not working for you and whether you're feeling better or not?
- And do you get a sense of being really listened to and heard and that their esoteric theories are not getting in the way?

Before I finish here, please allow me a little puff for myself and my Feelbetter Counselling practice- I think you can answer yes to all these questions as they apply to my practice. Unlike any other private therapist that I know I keep a rigorous track record of how all my clients progress with me by asking them to fill in the short form at the beginning of every therapy session. This shows an 85% record of success, which is very high.

Additionally I certainly convey a strong expectation that you will get better and this is credible by my manner, by my evidence, by how I explain what I do and then do it and by the close therapeutic relationship that we will establish.

8. The best way on how to treat depression?

It is really quite hard to convey the degree of ignorance, pseudoscience and special pleading which lies at the heart of the psychiatric and medical profession when it comes to how they deal with depression. And in what I am about to say, you can be excused for thinking that I must be exaggerating. But I'm not.

I'm still waiting to discover in all my reading, in all my viewing of websites and listening to people talking on YouTube and the like -- a credible theory of what a depression is and why people succumb to it – that makes any sense at all. Yes there is a lot out there – but when you look at it, it just disappears in your hand, like a piece of rotten fruit. So, there is a lot about symptoms and behaviours – of low mood, loss of motivation, absence of pleasure, isolation and shame and a lack of purpose and meaning. And there will be lots on risk factors. For example did you know those with cancer are susceptible to depression. Now there's a surprise! Or that unemployment is not good for your mood and self confidence. Well thanks a lot for that. But if you ask what is the overriding biological/neurobiological explanation or theory that fits it altogether? I promise you will be disappointed.

And that is why the ideas that I have been expanding here and on my websites not only makes sense but are so exciting. Of the role of dreaming and useless rumination and getting needs met and vicious circles leading to mental and emotional exhaustion..... and all the rest. And it takes the argument to a new higher-level - to a level that will make sense to those who suffer from or have ever suffered from depression.

And let me be clear - the ideas that I have been expressing here and on my websites are not mine. They are based on the Human Givens and of course my answer to the question what is the best way on how to treat depression is to use the principles and approach of the Human Givens and so find a qualified and experienced Human Givens practitioner. And there are enough of us around in the UK for you to find someone. We are all on the Human Givens register of fully qualified practitioners.

Let me say a few words about what Human Givens is about. It is a little more than 15 years old, is UK based and was started by two guys - Ivan Tyrell and Joe Griffin. They remain the main originators and teachers still. They have created a magnificent literature, they have formulated a programme that trains excellent therapists and they have put together both original work (much of it around dreaming) and a brilliant synthesis of the best from the past. They purport to provide not just good counselling teaching but a new bio psycho social model of what is to be human – grand claims I know, but justified in my opinion. (see chapter 23)

The key insight is this: that human beings, because they are living creatures have emotional needs that they must get met to be mentally healthy and if any of these needs are not met, then they will suffer distress. It therefore follows that if a human being is not using their resources properly and particularly their emotional resources such that they are not living a life where they are getting their needs met - then they will suffer mental problems notably around depression and anxieties and addictive behaviours.

And so to help people who are suffering particularly in this case from depression, you have to understand the psychology of it, heal resources and get people problem-solving to get their life working again. Sounds pretty straightforward when it's put like that and actually if you know what you're doing it is not nearly as difficult as many people would say. Which is why I am a depression recovery optimist?

9. What are the signs of depression in women?

The important point is not that women's depressions are different from men – my experience is that they are identical – in the main driven by rumination, dreaming too much and a life that is just not working and cannot be made to work. The point is that women suffer much more from depression than men. This is well known and my own practice confirms it. For my depressed clients I see there is a split of three to one in favour of woman compared to men and having checked the stats, this seems to be the spilt nationally as well – up to 3 to 1 in favour of women.

I should say in parenthesis that I see approximately equal numbers of men and woman – but men come with different problems. So while perhaps a third of my female clients will be depressed and another third enduring anxieties of some kind – for men it is almost exactly reversed. Only a relatively small number of men will come to me with a classic depression and rather more with anxieties (a similar number to women) and a lot (at least a third) with addictions of some kind. And this concentration of addictions as a male response to a life that is not working or cannot be made to work also fits in with national trends. The national figures show that around 75% of addictive behaviours are male.

And there are good reasons for these differences - that are rooted in the differences between female and male brains.

Women use both sides of the brain when processing information whereas men use predominantly their left brain. Consequently men are more focused on facts and women will remember more about the emotional content. Women are more in touch with their own feelings and therefore interested in the feelings of others while men will analyse and remember more factual information. Men are problem solvers – "this is what they do" while women look to see and prefer to talk. Now there's a surprise.

Women will tend to talk through problems or situations reaching their conclusion by sharing and empathic responses. Men prefer to think through things alone and clarify their options before discussing. You can see the origins of much marital and partner discord here – with women likely to accuse a man of not listening when he offers advice and solutions and men will resent suggestions that he needs to talk when he wants time alone to think.

The key point being that the female way of dealing with their problems – if it fails to work will quite naturally feed into depression. Women are ruminators and are open to the idea that talking through their problems will sort them out. It also explains why around 80% of the counselling profession comprise women.

But talking will not help if depression exhaustion is setting in. In fact it will make the situation worse – by feeding useless rumination. So then women must go against their natural instincts and if you like become more male – to understand that they need their problem of exhaustion to be sorted and quickly too.

Before finishing, let me say a word about post natal depression – the classic female only depression, but in my experience no different than other depressions. The important observation is that the birth of a child can lead to major stresses for the mother. Being responsible for a new born, perhaps isolated and exhausted and possibly having to deal with problematic relationships. And so on. And if all of these cannot be resolved and so the new mother begins to worry and panic then she will, in all likelihood, drift into a depression.

We don't have a distinctive "I have been dumped by my girlfriend" depression and my experience in helping depressed young mothers is that it does no good to do likewise with their depressions.

10. What are the signs of depression in men?

In some ways, depression is more serious for men than women, even though it is less common in men. This reflects the differences between male and female brains that were covered in the previous chapter (chapter 9). Men are problem solvers and less given to worrying and rumination for the sake of it. So if they find themselves depressed because they are worrying too much and sleeping badly and their life is not working however hard they try, then they are more likely to look for the ultimate solution - which is of course suicide.

National statistics show that in the UK men are 3 1/2 times more likely to commit suicide than women. Women attempt suicide more often than men but they are much more likely to fail. Is this because they are not problem solvers like men or that these attempts are cries for help and so not so serious? Probably it is a bit of both.

I think also that this difference in brain function between men and women is the reason why addictions are far more common in men than women. I quoted statistics that over seven in ten of all addictive behaviours were by men. Because of course an addiction is a form of self medication and can be seen as an attempt at a solution to a problem. Hardly ideal of course and often this will feed into depressive symptoms as hope fade and confidence collapses. Then the depression can be an element of an addiction or vice versa. This is quite rare for women in my experience.

What else do we know about men's brains and their contrast with women's? Well, men need greater stimulus to start on a project and then they will then take more risks and welcome deadlines and competition. They are also more comfortable with status and are always looking to find the pecking order and are then happy with their place in it - much more than women who are much more interested in notions of equality. This could perhaps explain why men have tended to achieve more senior positions than women who are more risk averse, less competitive and prefer to work as part of a team. Women are less focused on doing one thing at a time so can appear to achieve less, although as we have seen they will be more aware of what is happening with the people around them on an emotional level.

When stressed or upset men are also more likely to become angry - and this often has an addictive quality as anger can be quite exciting and relieving. But of course if the anger gets out of control such that aspects of a man's life are being seriously affected particularly around their important family relationships - then a depression can easily follow. And my experience is that anger is very rarely an element in a woman's depression.

11. Depression UK - what is depression?

We are told that we are living through a depression epidemic in the West and for sure the statistics are frightening. Antidepressant prescriptions are rising at an exponential rate and if the figures to be believed are more than doubling every 15 years or so. In America antidepressant prescriptions have risen by 400% in the past 20 years. In the UK last year (2013) there were 50 million prescriptions - that's right 50 million which is close to the adult population. And we hear authoritative voices saying that one in four of us will be experiencing a depression at least once in our lifetime and so on and so forth. Vested interests are demanding more and more money and more and more resources on the back of this – on the unspoken assumption of course that they know how to relieve this industrial scale depression epidemic.

What is going on? The fact that depression has exploded in the past 40 years or so is a further indicator that depression cannot be an illness in the accepted meaning of that word. Yes a disabling condition like a twisted ankle, but not an illness surely. And it is noteworthy also that the older generation - those that were born before the Second World War have never shared in this depression epidemic.

To my mind, this confirms the view that depression is not something that the medical profession and the medical mindset should have anything to do with. And if there is a depression epidemic under way then it has to be to social, political and economic factors that we have to look to.

And of course if we go down that route, there are a plethora of possible explanations for this depression epidemic. Who could doubt for example the following as highly significant social changes in the UK?

The first is that work is much less certain as there are no longer jobs for life in industries that are desperate for people. Families are much less integrated between the generations and the standard family unit is being continually undermined - both practically and ideologically. We rely much more on the state to deal with our problems - of our physical health, and mental health of course, our living standards and to protect us from individual and social crises and so on. Indeed there is an industry, financed by the taxpayer that is designed just to identify problems and to suggest high spending solutions to be rolled out nationwide.

Further, the rate of change of everything has speeded up - of technology, of communication, of connectedness and so on. Is it surprising that stress levels remain high despite affluence and that we look increasingly outside ourselves and those of our families and immediate communities for resolution?

The UK is participating in this western phenomenon with the pharmaceutical industry all too ready to oblige.

My honest instinct, though I can't prove it is to believe that the epidemic is not nearly on the scale that it is believed to be, that the antidepressants that are prescribed are not there to deal with depression and anxieties as I would understand and that instead it is just a feature of the age we live in. A hundred and fifty years ago middle-class houses were quite rare and each had servants. Now they are much more plentiful and each has a bathroom cabinet full of antidepressants.

12. Who can I trust to help me with my Depression?

Depression is emotional and mental exhaustion - that drains all capacity to take the necessary action to live a life that works and can literally drive you into the ground. All depressed people worry too much and unproductively and eventually this fills their heads such that they can do little else but worry. This in turn increases the amount that they have to dream as they try so very hard but unsuccessfully to clear all of those worries and fears. And so depressed people fall into a vicious circle when nothing seems to work. And as their mood gets more and more fearful and low, they lose all sense of pleasure and meaning in life and so they tend to hide away rather than engage. And for all depressed people, self confidence is at rock bottom because of course their life is not working and they don't know what to do about it or more accurately - when everything they do does not work.

I would say that the first thing that you need when you are looking for somebody to trust who can help with your depression is to find someone who has an understanding of what you're going through that makes as much sense as this.

If in contrast, and in answer to the question about what is depression and why I should trust you, you find a person who hides behind platitudes, then I would turn and go elsewhere. And what are the platitudes that many will speak? That depression a very serious mental illness and has many causes and it's all very difficult.

I would also be very suspicious of anybody who when talking about depression just talked of symptoms - such as low mood, loss of motivation and libido, bad temper and irritability and wishing to be alone and so on and so forth. Because of course that person is saying nothing of any substance – is she? I'm afraid you will find so many who hide behind these platitudes and descriptions of symptoms. It seems to me that this is mainly an indicator of their ignorance.

I would also be pretty suspicious of anybody who is too quick to suggest antidepressants, because that is the ultimate scatter gun approach to depression fuelled by ignorance and powerful big Pharma vested interests. Yes antidepressants can work but then again they can make you feel worse. And sometimes depressants can have significant side effects, but then again they might not. And sometimes antidepressants create dependence that can then require time to come off them and sometimes they don't. And sometimes, if antidepressants help they do so for a long time and then sometimes the beneficial effect will fade away. Nobody can know in advance. It's just a crap shoot and there is a better way

The truth is that you must accept that there is extraordinary ignorance out there. Of course if you are depressed that is the last thing that you need to hear. But it means that there must be confidence by you in the competence and experience of the person you're going to go to for help. And if you have that then you have undoubtedly reached first base.

13. Why is just talking about your problems never enough on its own?

If you are full to bursting, then it makes sense to let it all out. Who could argue with that? If you are depressed and your head is going round and round with all kinds of theories and explanations as to why you are feeling so bad and if you have urgent problems to sort out – money worries, jobs, relationships etc. etc. – then surely you need to talk to someone about it and quickly too? It seems so obvious doesn't it? That you should talk to friends or family or even to one of the legion of counsellors out there who are trained to listen.

Well no. Talking is the last thing depressed people should do.

It is really very simple and follows as night follows day from understanding what a depression is. You will now know that a depression is the exhaustion caused by worrying and ruminating too much. Depression is an exhausted brain that is dreaming too much in a failing attempt to clear all of the exhaustion and over worrying.

Depression people are trapped in their thoughts and emotions and quite naturally they want to unload to any who might listen. But this will only give short-term relief and could in fact just feed the rumination as fuel feeds a flame. Yes there will be real problems to sort out – but before even attempting to sort them out, your head needs to be in a much better shape.

That is maybe my main message.

Imagine someone who twisted their ankle and, being desperately concerned that she might never walk again, keeps walking and walking, even though this was making her ankle even worse. What would you say to her? It would surely be that she should rest it and to only begin walking again when the ankle was stronger. The same applies to depression. Calm you mind, worry less and only tackle your problems when your mind is fitter.

Imagine if you are being asked to talk about your feelings – and they are overwhelming and chaotic and unordered and inescapable? Even if you are being asked by someone trained to listen. It does not help to translate these chaotic and overwhelming feelings into words and thoughts when they are so strong (as they are for all locked in a depression trance).

It is difficult enough to make a decent translation from the Russian of Chekov into English. Imagine how much more difficult it would be for someone trapped in their emotions to attempt anything worthwhile by way of a translation – of these feelings into mere words?

No – get arousal down by action and distraction and by a deep understanding of why these feelings are so overwhelming. Only then begin to listen to what your feelings might be saying and maybe then it might be worthwhile talking about them.

14. Why is the NHS so unsatisfactory for depression?

Do you recall the scorpion story.

"A scorpion and a frog meet on the bank of a stream and the scorpion asks the frog to carry him across on its back. The frog asks, "How do I know you won't sting me?" The scorpion says, "Because if I do, I will die too."

The frog is satisfied, and they set out, but in midstream, the scorpion stings the frog. The frog feels the onset of paralysis and starts to sink, knowing they both will drown, but has just enough time to gasp "Why?"

Replies the scorpion: "It's my nature…"

What if the nature of the NHS is such that however hard it tries, it just can never help with our nationwide depression epidemic or much more important with your depression?

Let's consider our dear old NHS? It is first and foremost a medical delivery organisation - set up to deliver medical methods and procedures that can be rolled out nationwide. And for hip replacements and emergency stroke treatment and child immunisation and much else, the NHS can deliver. Like McDonald's hamburgers, the same medical treatment will, broadly speaking, be in Inverness as in Doncaster as in Cornwall as anywhere.

And what does this mean? First that all the conditions it deals with are deemed to be medical and so they must be pathologised first - so they can be diagnosed and then a standardised treatment applied. Medically trained doctors are uncomfortable with non-medical phenomena such as the mind/body connection, placebo as an aid to healing - they see them more as a con trick to be dismissed and overruled. They are most comfortable with scientific criteria – randomised control trials, peer reviewed studies and so on and so forth.

Finally of course the NHS is a political football – and so at the forefront of political debate and point scoring and sides taking.

And how does depression fit in? What if depression is not an illness? That there is no virus, no bacteria, no physical phenomena, no biology, no medical tests that identify depression and this is after 100 years of trying? What if there are no silver bullets, no active ingredients no formulas or procedures that can be proved to assist recovery from depression?

What if the delivery of depression counselling can never be standardised? What if there is no single counselling approach that has ever been proven to be better than any other? And horror of horrors, what if some counsellors are better than others. And that these good counsellors need to be allowed to get on and do their stuff?

Finally what if this depression epidemic that we are told we are living through is much better explained by social and economic change and the speed of technology and the change in family and community and the growing size of the state and so on and so forth?

What then for the NHS and its attempts to deal with depression? The answer is obvious - the NHS will not be able to cope because it has to go against its nature. Like the scorpion.

So the NHS tries and tries to standardise and to medicalise because that is what it does. And whatever cunning schemes the NHS comes up with and the billions that it spends - nothing seems to work. And the incidence of depression continues to grow and grow and grow.

15. Why do people get depressed?

It's all about their journey - by which I mean the journey of their life. How well they were equipped at the beginning is a factor but much more important is what happened to them on that journey and how they reacted to that and where that reaction led.

It's always about the journey and how well that journey leaves us equipped or not to live a life that works right now. At one extreme there will be people who started life well and found that their experiences through life supported and developed them rather than broke them so their life has been one where their needs have been reasonably well or very well met. These people will not be suffering mental distress and will not be depressed.

But then there are others - who have not been well prepared in their early life and perhaps additionally have experienced great difficulties and unfortunate life circumstances - even trauma. And in consequence, they have struggled to create a life that works and so will be enduring stress and strain and mental problems that for many will end in depression.

And once you start down a road that is not working and you do not know how to escape, then things will unravel. I have talked about vicious circles where one difficulty leads to another in reaction to it and so on. And we also know that a vicious circle will be amplified by rumination and excessive and exhausting dreaming which then directly leads to depression.

In this very brief summary I want to emphasise the great significance of trauma or near trauma experiences. Trauma is so much more common than is commonly believed. For example, more than half my depressed clients will have some kind of trauma memory that needs to be cleared before real progress can be made.

The great news is though that I can clear most traumatic memories using trance methods. Indeed all Human Givens therapists are taught how to do this and we have amazing success in doing this.

Let me give you some examples about what I mean. Over the last year for my seriously depressed clients, I have successfully de-traumatised memories of school bullying, a father who drank far too much, the divorce of parents, childhood experience of leaving a family home and going somewhere strange and frightening, being dumped by a boyfriend, a period of very stressful unemployment and finally, powerful memories of a previous depression.

In dealing with difficult circumstances, people have to tell themselves a story that makes sense and often this story is one where they are the guilty party, the failure and so on. And this leads to black-and-white thinking, a bias towards negativity and a focus on what is wrong and bad.

This means that in my third stage of recovery (after hope has been restored and firefighting has reduced arousal and improved sleep), healing is about shifting the focus towards the recognition of resources, of where there is good experiences and memories and where lessons can be learned after which we can all move on.

Life can deal us all difficult circumstances and resilience is then vital. Another way therefore to understand how to heal in this third stage of recovery, when you are building or rebuilding a life that works is to understand how resilience can be developed. And a lot of my work with clients is about doing just this.

16. Why are anti-depressants not the answer for me?

More and more of us are using antidepressants - in the UK alone there were around 50 million prescriptions last year which is equal to the entire adult population. That's right equal to the UK population. By comparison, it appears psychological help and counselling is in decline. I saw figures recently for the USA which showed a decline of over a third in 10 years.

My answer to make sense of this is to argue that neither antidepressants nor the counselling and psychotherapy that is typically on offer is much good in dealing with depression. And as we have a depression epidemic right now with no signs of control I think we can safely say that I am probably right about this - that neither antidepressants nor the typical counselling psychotherapy can be much good.

So what can be said about antidepressants? I've used the phrase scattergun when it comes to antidepressants and that really is the best way to see them. That if you do take them you will really have no idea whether they will be good for you or bad or for how long they will help or what the side effects might be and the difficulties there might be in coming off them. This is the best summary I've come across of what the evidence says – from the Human Givens institute.

"Anti-depressants work in aggregate about as well as placebo which means about one third of people benefit. But of course they do not pretend to treat the root cause and so there is a high rate of

relapse. And a quarter of users will do less well than placebo."

And there are unquestionably side effects – from an increased suicide risk, loss of sex drive, dizziness, nausea, fatigue, headaches and so on Finally, a third of those taking anti-depressants will suffer withdrawal symptoms."

To summarise – I am not saying that for all depressed individuals, antidepressants are useless or bad for you. And I have had clients who swear by them, though not very many. What I am saying is that the right kind of talking therapy – namely Human Givens – is a much better option.

17. Why is most counselling, including Cognitive Behavioural Therapy, such hard work?

From where I stand there are two main problems with most forms of counselling and psychotherapy as they attempt to deal with depression. The first is that no counselling approach (and this includes CBT) actually understands what a depression is and so all they can do is focus on depression symptoms. The idea that depression is fuelled by exhausting over dreaming which means that our minds are unable to think or feel straight (which is what Human Givens believes) means that traditional therapy is bound to be at best ineffective. It's like putting an exclusively Dutch speaker into the middle of China and expecting that person to thrive. It's possible in principle but will be very hard

The second reason is that the tools used are barely adequate for the task. There is traditional talking therapy which just talks (as it says on the tin) and which makes no use of hypnotherapy or trance. But if as Human Givens believes, the key aspects that need to be dealt with in the depressed person is their use of and sensitivity to their emotions - how can this be done if the emotions are so strong that they can only be accessed at the deepest trance level?

And this also explains why CBT is so difficult. It begins from the idea that it is bad thoughts that are the problem. So CBT is about complex methods and principles to confront thoughts which don't help - such as "I am no good and everybody hates me" or "everything always goes wrong in my life" and so on. But what if these thoughts are driven by the abject despair of an exhausted brain? How exactly can these thoughts be challenged in a meaningful way? I would say it's like cutting the lawn with a pair of scissors or emptying out a bath with a spoon- really hard work and pretty ineffective, to put it mildly.

The other problem with CBT is that now big vested interests are involved. Lots of people earn a living from it in some way or other - either directly from the NHS or by approval from the NHS. This means it is very difficult to be critical as it will be attacked regardless. And this is despite a recent study which shows that the government IAPT program which means improving access to psychological therapies - which is the vehicle for rolling out CBT across the nation has proved to be seriously ineffective - helping just one in 10 of those who sign up.

One reason for this maybe that by expanding so quickly, the quality of the therapists in very poor in IAPT and as we know, it is the quality of the therapist and not the model of therapy that is the really important thing.

Another interesting phenomenon with regard to CBT is that the basis of CBT is always expanding. There is now mindfulness CBT and trauma release CBT and one-day no doubt there will be Human Givens CBT. It is the name that counts today and CBT must be somewhere in the title.

There are many excellent therapists out there including CBT and traditional - and some will be able to help you with your depression. But so many will start from a pretty poor base - of depression ignorance and poor training.

18. Is Depression an illness that needs me to trust my GP and the NHS?

What is an illness? Is a twisted ankle an illness or a cut finger? If you were wheeled into A&E from a motorway pileup on the M25 - would you be ill then? And if you had perforated your lung in addition to breaking bones in that car accident? Would that be different in some way?

It's a tough one and for most of us there are no clear cut answers. I would say that an illness is definitely more than just a body malfunction of some kind especially if it has been caused by events in our daily life - such as going over on our ankle on a paving stone in the street or even by eating too much sugar or cream cakes perhaps

And what of genetic problems such as Down's syndrome or autism or even Alzheimer's and Parkinson's? I think many of us would think these might possibly be understood as illnesses if some biological link can be made.

I think it is hard to sustain the illness argument if you cannot point to some biological or chemical connection which directly feeds into the operation of the body. In other words you are making some kind of body mind distinction, which you can certainly do for smallpox or the common cold.

But heart disease caused by a tightening of the arteries? Is this an illness?

Regardless of how you answer these questions, it is

surely very difficult to argue that depression is an illness in any of these accepted senses. Yet many argue without any evidence I hasten to add that there is a genetic component and scientists have established a connection between how the brain works when someone is depressed. But of course this doesn't prove causation - as a bruised and swollen ankle say nothing about the cause of it.

Did you know that even after 100 years trying, there has been no biological or chemical marker for any so-called mental illness and certainly no medical test? And this goes for depression as well as all the others such as schizophrenia, personality disorders, PTSD and so on. Indeed for all of these so-called mental illnesses psychiatrists talk only about symptoms and behaviours - pretending to be doctors if you like.

I don't believe depression is an illness in the sense that it is amenable to treatment by medically trained personnel. Yes, medically trained people can deal with a broken leg and a perforated lung as they understand the mechanics of the body. And they can also be there for you if you have a cancerous growth or serious physical disability such as MS (perhaps).

But what about depression with social factors and lifetime stresses and dealing with trauma and worrying and so dreaming too much? An illness? No way

19. I seem to have been depressed for most of my life – it must surely be an illness?

Well yes it's easy to believe that - to put in the box marked "What is this?" and call it an illness. But when you say illness you are not really saying anything are you? Because illnesses are quite hard to define as we have seen in the previous chapter (chapter 18). Illnesses certainly imply some kind of physical malady for which there is a medical cause and which will admit of a medical resolution. And I'm afraid on both counts most of the depressions that people suffer from having no obvious physical nature or indicator and there is certainly no medical treatment which would pass the basic medical tests that apply to physical illnesses.

To put this in perspective and so you can understand that even after many years of suffering from depression, it does not mean that it cannot be resolved by the standard means that I have been discussing. I can think of four reasons.

The first is of course that the depressed mind is exhausted and cannot think straight. The second is that a depression that extends over many years will almost certainly have some early trauma that is still a source of debilitation and vulnerability - and it is to the resolution of this that one needs to look. The third reason is that you have not had an experience of recovery that has stayed with you - that there is a hole where good memories need to be or (to put it another way) you will have no realisation that even a small change can set you off in a better direction.

And what is my final reason? It is that by simply understanding what a depression is - by reading this book and looking at my websites and by following some of the links, you will understand the connection between excessive and pointless rumination to over dreaming and your depression. And by knowing how the brain generates a depression, you will know far more than most about what a depression is all about - and certainly more than the medical practitioner that you might be tempted to visit.

Just a few weeks ago I saw a woman of 73 years who had been depressed on and off for the whole of her life. What we found when we worked together was there was still a terrifying active and alive memory of something that happened to her when she was six years old - the horror of going to boarding school some 67 years ago. And so we cleared that trauma in trance and now she is at last clear of her depression.

Let me tell you of another client. She is in her mid-50s and she could go back to her memories of depression in the 1980s when she was a young woman. And all of that time ever since until very recently she would say that she has been depressed. But what we discovered as we worked together was that for all of that time she just could not live the kind of life that she needed to live. She was without a long-term companion or partner and she was doing a job (as a teacher) that she realised that she hated. She had been a regular taker of ante-depressants over many years and over this time she felt that she could not have done without them. And when we worked together it never occurred to me that I should challenge that belief that her antidepressants did take the edge off her depression. But the good news is that she's no longer depressed. For the first time for 30 years is doing a job she likes she has activities and hobbies which give her real pleasure and that is enough.

So even after a lifetime, change is possible and your depression can become a thing of the past

20. Want to know the three steps to depression recovery?

I'm sure you do want to know so here they are. And let me just say by way of introduction that all I am saying here reflects the practical lessons I have learnt as a successful depression recovery therapist.

The first step is to build hope because almost without exception depressed people lack hope. They live in a state of exhausted despair where nothing they do seems to work and where the future seems very dark. And what I have found is that for most of my depressed clients, the best way to build hope is to explain as clearly as possible what a depression is and why they are feeling as they are feeling. The purpose is for them to realise and for you to realise also that you're not going mad that you do not have a serious illness and that small persistent changes will make a permanent difference. You can see how hopeful this can be and if it is followed by the second stage of fire fighting (which I will come onto the moment) then what happens is that my clients have a direct experience that what I'm saying to them is actually what they are discovering for themselves.

There are times when hope is built more directly than that by giving a direct experience of being calmer in trance – but normalising, or explaining is the best way.

The second step is what I call fire fighting. What I mean by this is short-term and immediate help to reduce rumination and so improve sleep and dreaming and so build and replace a little energy and clarity. Clearly this second step follows on very closely from the first step because if some hope is restored, then this will itself reduce useless rumination and open my clients to taking the necessary early steps to get sleep and dreaming under control.

The third stage is what I have called partnership. This is a joint endeavour between my client and me to get their life working better. Because somewhere down the line there will be problems that need to be dealt with or have emerged as the depression has taken hold. These may be very practical around decisions to be taken regarding work or training, friendships or relationships or it can be more profound. I will certainly be looking to see if there is trauma that needs to be cleared. I will also be looking to change the focus of my clients towards their strengths and to possibilities that they might have believed are closed off to them. What I often find is that as my clients calm down, this third stage can be largely done by them. Sometimes but not always in which case it may be that thinking styles need to be worked on and resources and emotional patterns need to be shifted. (See chapter 25 for client recovery stories)

What I often find in this third stage is that the narrative or story of the life that my client is telling themselves is too negative, stuck and problematic. They cannot see a progression and that they are learning lessons and able moving forward. So I may very well spend time on this. This third step is of course where good therapy often begins (chapter 22).

I am not saying that these three steps need to be

followed sequentially 1 2 and 3. For sometimes I will have to mix them up. But remember all three are vital for recovery – building hope, fire fighting and a partnership. You must have hope and believe that you will get better. You must do whatever it takes to feel less exhausted and more in control. And finally to regain or to maintain good emotional health, you must get a life that works for you.

21. What's the best depression help I can get?

This is a leading question of course, because the only answer is me, obviously! But assuming that you know that, let me expand a little on the Human Givens approach – which has taught me the biology and psychology of what a depression is, has taught me skills and practical tools for developing my counselling practice and by virtue of magnificent literature and wisdom has provided me with an understanding of what it is to be human that makes so much sense and I use every day. (see chapter 23)

What that means is that you should look for a Human Givens trained practitioner as your first port of call for help with your depression. I'm afraid to say that Human Givens is more or less unknown outside the UK but of course I am available to Skype

Human Givens is UK based and is still only 15 years old. The two originators and still the main teachers of Human Givens are Joe Griffin and Ivan Tyrell - inspirational teachers and writers who over the years have put together a unique teaching programme, a literature of excellent books that covers self help, technical research and inspirational big pictures on the bio psychosocial theory of being human.

I would encourage all my readers to check them out. There is literature from Human Givens Publishing, courses from Human Givens College and the main website - the Human Givens Institute.

You should begin to understand their work by reading of the Human Givens organising idea of what is to be human. That we have essential emotional needs and a guidance system (namely our resources, particularly our emotional resources) that we use to get these essential needs met. If we do that successfully then we are mentally and emotionally healthy. But if we fail because of circumstances, weaknesses in our resources and so on, then we will suffer mental and emotional distress. And many people in ignorance call these mental illnesses, but actually they are no such thing.

It is impossible to do justice to Human Givens in this short chapter. But let me just say this in addition. Much of what Human Givens teach about what it is to be human and what makes excellent counselling comes from their knowledge of what has been said before them. Griffin and Tyrell are magnificent synthesisers - that thanks to them I am standing on the shoulders of many giants that came before. I am thinking in particular of the work of Milton Erickson, Indries Shah, Arthur Deikman, Daniel Goleman and many more

There is now hard evidence published in a peer reviewed journal (by the British Psychological Society in 2011) that HG trained therapists in the NHS do a much better job than the norm.

As I have said, there are lots of tips and techniques and advice out there for are those suffering from depression. And there is no doubt that exercises is useful, good nutrition will be a help and a mindfulness/meditation practice can be important. But for most people suffering from depression, these are complements that should never be the main story. The main story is the Human Given's theory of depression. And to give just one example, the idea that someone lost in fearful and exhausting depression could even begin a mindfulness practice from a standing start is laughable.

PART 2

ARTICLES FROM THE DEPRESSION OPTIMIST

CHAPTER 22

GOOD THERAPY – HOW COUNSELLING WORKS

These are from my Depression Help Blog and set down the counselling principles by which I work.

a) My two beginning principles for mental and emotional relief

b) What makes good counselling – two simple truths

c) How Feelbetter Counselling works – to open doors

d) Building Positive Expectancy

e) What is Normalisation and why am I so keen on it?

f) Be wise not clever – cultivate intuition

g) Are we hard wired or flexibly webbed?

h) Life stories and time lines – as they slowly crept up on me

i) Using the Rewind method to clear trauma

j) Examples of Trauma relieved as a prelude to healing and recovery

k) Want to understand and relieve Depression – then focus on Emotions and not Thoughts?

a) My two beginning principles for mental and emotional relief

Emotional and mental healing is not about fixing something, like a hot water boiler or even a broken leg, but setting a living being free to move in a better direction. There is a story to be told of how each individual who now finds themselves in serious distress got where they are and over time coped or failed to cope with what was going wrong and what was happening – and of vicious circles that took them further away from emotional health. So, we can all be inspired by the words of Milton Erickson, the father of modern hypnotherapy. "Therapy is often a matter of tipping the first domino" and "People do not come into therapy to change their past but their future." Gabrielle Roth also understood "If you just set people in motion they'll heal themselves."

Luckily, there are many ways to do this and certainly many ways I attempt to do so. But in all cases, there is one overriding and immediate objective for virtually all clients who come to me – which is to get their emotional arousal down and more under their control. Think of a ship tossing in a storm. The sea has to quieten down before anything else is possible. The same will be true for those who come to me, whatever are the particulars of their problem. Their emotions will be out of control – dominated by fears, obsessive thoughts, exhaustion, angers, shame and guilt and so on. And as a result, their self confidence will have plummeted and they will be stuck and lost. And movement, even a small one will be very hard.

To understand the importance of tipping the first domino and getting arousal down explains why normalisation and positive expectancy is so important for my therapy.

Both can set a new direction by building hope. Believe me!

b) What makes good counselling – two simple truths

There are hundreds of therapy models out there and if you go to any respectable counselling directory website, you will see the current favourites – counsellors or psychotherapists trained in person centred, integrative, psychoanalytic, gestalt and the current big daddy cognitive behavioural therapy or CBT.

But how to choose which model is best for you?

I am assuming that you do not have an attachment to any approach. You just know you need help and want to feel better. So which is the best? It's a simple question. Or maybe you are a public agency (say the NHS) and you have an entire nation of depressed people that you have been mandated to treat and you need to find the counselling model that will offer the best value and do the most good for what money is available?

But how to you choose? Because one of these therapy models must be best. Right? We successfully search for the fastest sprinter, the best cancer treatment, the winning football team, the best political party, the most efficient car, the prettiest woman, the most handsome actor, the latest and best tooth whitener? So what is the best model – meaning the model that will get me (or the nation) feeling better more reliably and efficiently that any of the others. There must be one. Right?

Well no – wrong.

The Dodo bird verdict. Do you vaguely remember the Dodo bird from Alice's Adventures in Wonderland. He who said "Everybody has won and all must have prizes." Counselling is like that – everybody wins because they are all equally good. No one model has ever been proven to be better than any of the others. They all do some good and are better than nothing, but based on mountains of research from all over the world, for all kinds of models of therapy in all kinds of circumstances, the result is always the same. Yes ALWAYS. Everyone must have prizes.

So if you are looking for the model that is best, you will never find it. And neither will the NHS.

But there is a second truth that the research also shows to be true. It is that some therapists are better than others. It is not the model that counts but the counsellor.

Now this is a devastating and profound conclusion and flies in the face of so much that we believe instinctively and unthinkingly to be true.

c) How Feelbetter Counselling works – to open doors

The prime importance of normalising – i.e. having a credible explanation of why your client feels as she does and to establish a positive expectancy of beneficial change – such that both of us (client and therapist) are open to using our resources to facilitate the movement that is needed. Then two starting principles – of looking for that tipping point or setting up a motion or movement and to work in the first instance to get arousal down.

After this the focus can then widen – as doors become visible and roads ahead become clearer. All of these essentially shift attention towards supporting a better emotional response to where clients find themselves – both more empowering and involving more useful action. It is as if the therapist's purpose is to lead to as many doors as possible that can be opened by the choice and instinct of the client. And there are so many doors.

In many ways, this is all about attention and refocusing.

Thus, attention can be directed to the useful resources and strengths the client may have and their most useful memories and away from those that are doing so much damage. And further, to focus on new interpretations (or stories) of the past – that attend on real or newly constructed experiences of resolution of problems and achievement and more balanced explanations, with many shades of grey rather than too much black and white. Motivations may also be tweaked towards better action or away from action that damages. And so on.

Reframing is at the heart of what the redirection of attention is about and is perhaps the best way to summarise the purpose of all of this heavyweight therapeutic attention shifting. What is needed is a shift or reframe that will facilitate an understanding and interpretation to events that prompts an emotional response that assists better action.

The indirect language of Milton Erickson is designed just for this – presupposing the desired outcome, embedding a helpful suggestion within other words, linking desired change to truisms (and so implying a causal link), double binds and concentrating on positive and congratulatory language and focus.

Attention shifting for many will also be facilitated by metaphors and stories. The therapist may be gently leading the patient or client but the patient is following willingly and with curiosity and openness. You can see what Roth was getting at when she said "If you just set people in motion they'll heal themselves."

Finally, there is more to say on the metaphors that work for depression, on the questions to ask and reframes to make, on the stories and the life narratives that can be so powerfully adapted, when de-traumatising is needed….and much more besides.

d) Building Positive Expectancy

The cultivation of positive expectancy is absolutely central to how I work – that both my client and I have an expectancy that he/she will get better. If it is there, then it will direct all necessary attention to my client's in built capacity to heal and into my wisdom and experience to find and use what is needed. There must be expectancy that healing is possible – for only then will the mind/body's healing and problem solving resources be activated. And to the extent that a client believes he/she will get better and has faith in my skills, experience and knowledge, then he/she is already at first base. We are talking of the placebo effect – or accessing the clients own natural unconscious expectation of beneficial change.

And how does this relate to rapport building or the establishment of a working alliance – which has long been understood as an essential pre-requisite for good counselling (and indeed any healing)? What I have found is that this can best be done by establishing a belief and expectation of improvement and recovery. Expectancy is pretty well equivalent to the essential requirement for rapport building, in my experience.

Of course, this expectation has to be credible. Clients can rarely be fooled as we are talking about subtle body language, an unconscious tone of voice as much as anything else. And if it is to be cultivated effectively, it must be real. This is the main reason why I have put such effort into my website and why I keep hard evidence of my progress (or lack of progress) at every session of therapy with every client. It also means that I must have full confidence in the Human Givens ideas as I have learnt and adapted to my own way of working.

And then, after there is some improvement, both my client and I can relax and feel a naturally growing confident expectation. On the other hand, if there is no improvement within a few sessions or it is not sustained, then it is absolutely critical that I remain calm and positive. This is to keep pressure off us both and so we can be open to whatever might be needed for healing. And if confidence is lost then so is positive expectancy and then the therapy is probably over.

After establishing the positive expectation of change, the requirement then widens to the shifting of all attention towards supporting a better emotional response. It is as if all doors can be opened. And there are so many doors.

e) What is Normalisation and why am I so keen on it?

What do I mean by Normalisation? It simply means the offering of a credible explanation of why one is feeling so bad. If normalisation does its job it will begin to take away the pressure of feeling culpable, guilty and ignorant, which is typically how depressed people feel (and indeed pretty well how all those in mental distress feel).

If normalisation does its job, then a more hopeful recovery mind-set can take root. Action to relieve the problem can begin to make sense and this can be owned by the sufferer.

If you think about it, you can see that so many of the posts in my feelbetter website and blog are essentially normalisation. You will get an explanation of why you are feeling so bad (if you are depressed right now) - and even if you were to think that maybe there might just be something in this explanation of depression – then that will lift some pressure off you.

Normalisation becomes a liberating reframe by providing an accessible and apparently sufficiently complete explanation for the endured mental problems – that not only makes sense but will accord with the experience of the sufferer. That it is normal and you are not going mad – that the terrible way you are feeling and the lack of emotional control that is being endured has a simple explanation that is rooted in the common psychology of us all.

So much of the anguish and pain of mental problems (notably for depression but for much else as well) arises because there is so much ignorance. Moreover, this ignorance extends well beyond the sufferer to include the common media explanations and up to and including most of the medical experts. The consequence of such widespread ignorance is to feed the fear and arousal that is causing the distress in the first place. Humans are programmed to be always asking the question "why" when they are feeling bad and then, depending how desperate they are, to alight on all manner of explanations, however unreasonable, improbable and unhelpful they may be.

There is another consequence of good normalisation – of an authoritative and credible explanation by a therapist of why someone is feeling so bad. And that is that the client and the therapist will begin to share a positive expectancy of recovery and relief. And if both do that, then recovery has taken a giant step forward.

f) Be wise not clever – cultivate intuition

We have been talking of the uncomfortable truth that good healers and clinicians are not good, primarily because of the model and method that they follow. That there is something else – an x factor.

One can cultivate it. But what you don't do is pretend that you can learn it from a book. Marilyn vos Savant put it thus "To acquire knowledge she wrote, one must study; but to acquire wisdom, one must observe."

And this story, **the three fat fish** (by Rob Parkinson) is one of my favourites and puts it very well. The story illustrates the difference between wisdom (trusting your deep finely honed instincts), cleverness (trusting your brain to work something out) and stupidity (giving no thought to the future and hoping something will turn up)

Three fat fish lived in a deep hidden pool near a river bend: one was wise, the other was clever and the third was stupid. They were fat because they ran the show in their fairly hidden and protected pool and so any that visited – eels, insects, frogs, snake and of course other fish – they could eat. And then one day, three men found the pool – and as they approached one of them pointed out and spotted the fat lovely fish. And all of the fish could see that the men there pointing and excited. Now the wise fish acted immediately and without even saying goodbye, he was off – swimming to new places. And as did so he made a big splash and churned up the water in his rush to escape to waters new.

The clever fish, who also realised that there was a problem thought – I am going to have to outwit these men. The stupid fish didn't really see that there was a problem – maybe the men had just come to watch he reasoned. And anyway, he could hide at the deepest bottom of the pool. Clever fish knew though that this was risky – that something more needed to be done – as the men could have nets that could trawl along the bottom of the pool, however deep it was. But the more clever fish thought, he just could not come up with a plan that seemed watertight (if you will pardon the expression). "How to act and when – that was the question? I must analyse this predicament very carefully – systematically separating out all of the variables, creatively scrutinise tactical possibilities; and dynamically evolve an escape strategy." And as he thinks, the deeper he sinks. At last he decides that he needs information so he goes to inspect the inlet from the river. But when he got there he found that the men have covered this exit with some of their nets. The channel on the other side of the pond had also been covered he discovered as he swam across. "Damm" he says to himself.

Luckily though he was clever enough to remember that "Panic solves nothing." And "there is nothing like pressure to concentrate the mind." And sure enough he came up with a brilliant plan. So what clever fish does is bite up a huge glob of filthy mud and swirls it about his mouth. It's awful but he manages it. And then he swims back to the surface, rolls over all limp and floats as if dead.

And it works. One of the men notices clever fish floating, picks him up and smells him. "This one is dead and rotten" he shouts and throws clever fish onto the ground. Clever fish holds his breath and when the men are back at their work, he flips himself over and over until he reaches one of the channels beyond the netting, tumbles into the water with a smacking sound, spews the horrible mud and swims off to safety.

Stupid fish is asleep at the bottom of the pool until the net closes around him. Alas there is no escape for stupid fish and he ends up *providing a quite delicious supper for the men and their families.*

And later the men tell endless stories of the "Two Big Ones That Got Away" but nobody ever believes them.

g) Are we hard wired or flexibly webbed?

The brain is a metaphorical pattern matching organ. What this means is that we make sense of our daily experiences by relating it to what we have "stored" as past experiences. That what is happening now is similar in some way to a past memory and emotion?

When you think about it – pretty well all human progress is built on what has happened before. How can we (as individuals and societies) made sense of the present and how can we build on it to "progress" further? After all, we don't start from scratch each morning when we wake up.

This has to be a metaphorical recognition process. How is this like what happened before? So we are always on the lookout for similarities and connections in order to make sense of what is happening to us now.

And finally: how do we know that a metaphorical pattern match has been made? Well, by the emotion that we feel – that is the same as before.

This is why stories, metaphors, allegories, myths and pictures are so important for us.

And we can realise that the human brain is like a trembling web in the powerful metaphorical description of Ian Robertson in his Mind Sculpture. That everything that makes us who we are is embroidered in a trembling web of 100 billion brain cells. On average , each cell is connected 1000 times with other neurones, making a total of 100 000 billion connections. That there are more cell meeting points in the human brain than there are stars in the galaxy.

So not hard wired at all.

h) Life stories and time lines – as they slowly crept up on me

If I look back over my professional development as a Human Givens therapist, I can see so clearly how the idea of time lines have kept cropping up – so much so that I would say that their use has become an essential part of my therapeutic approach and increasingly explicitly.

While training, I attended an NLP workshop and experienced the power of walking (literally) back through your time line life and then forward again – so that it would feel different and easier in some way.

I remember learning that if an early event (a trauma in childhood say) was cleared, then like falling domino pieces the brain could reprocess subsequent events differently and more easily. This was so, as each experience depended on the previous. The result could be that a lifetime could begin to appear as altogether easier and more empowering. This was a powerful demonstration of the neurological truth that no memory is fixed or unchanging, like a computer file but is reconstituted every time you need it.

Right after learning this, I had the opportunity to work with a woman in her late fifties with a diagnosis of Borderline Personality Disorder. We went back to a bad early school experience which I cleared using rewind and then while she was in trance, we had a conversation that was me prompting her to revisit experiences that followed on from the early school memory and asking her how she could change them in some way – that would be better for her. We did this all the way up to her marriage in her mid-twenties.

The effect on her mental resilience and feelings of being in control were startling.

I then remember reading Jonathon Haidt's The Happiness Hypothesis. He talked of the need for all of us to have a narrative for our life which makes sense and from which we can see progression and movement – even from the very worst of times. He also suggested a writing exercise. This was that we can write down two stories – the life we have had and the life we might have had. For each story, we condense it into a sentence or phrase. I can vouch for the power of this exercise and how as a therapist, you can make use of the second story – to help build an altogether more empowering life narrative.

Finally I recall finding this website (www.timelinetherapy.net) and buying their teaching material. Though neither the website nor the download was quite to my taste, I got one very powerful idea. It was that you can move on from a bad time in your life (as long as it is not traumatic) when you have learnt its lesson. In other words, you can move on when the experience has been placed into a healthy narrative of your life.

Yes time lines – where would I be without them?

i) Using the Rewind method to clear trauma

Imagine yourself as a local GP, with a busy practice and only having ten minutes with each patient. And for the next week you could not prescribe antibiotics. Not at all! I imagine that it would be devastating for the GP. A great deal of confidence would drain away, as you would know that a vital means of quickly helping many of your patients would no longer be available. Like going naked into the conference room?

Well, if you told me that over the next week I could not use my normal trance methods and in particular could not use the Rewind method to clear the emotion around powerful memories from their past, I would be similarly drained.

Because I want to let you into a little secret – it is that around 75% of the clients I see, whether it for help with depression, anxieties of all kinds, addictions, diagnoses of personality disorder and so on or just having issues that need dealing with, will have some kind of trauma lurking somewhere in their past.

And so the knowledge that I can use Rewind to clear the trauma (or traumas) and that Rewind "works" nearly every time – well I think that is pretty amazing. OK I am experienced with Rewind now and can deal with abreactions and complications and also if my client does not have a very good visual memory. But knowing that this tool is there if I need it and that it will play a part in the recovery of up to three quarters of my clients (and I would guess for other Human Givens practitioners too) – well, that is an enormous comfort.

This leads me onto another point that links directly with how Human Givens sees mental illness. It is that most mental problems arise from a coping strategy that does not work. For example, we know that excessive and unproductive worrying will lead into depression. So imagine what it would be to live with trauma memories – with emotions, nightmares and avoidance etc. that arise without any means of control. It is clear that that could so easily unravel to makes one's life even worse.

It would be enough to make you "mentally ill"!

It also makes you wonder how therapists who purport to help with the mental problems of their clients manage to do so in the absence of any means to detraumatise – which of course is the situation for most counsellors, Cognitive Behavioural Therapists and psychiatrists. Probably like doctors before the discovery of antibiotics – i.e. not very well.

j) Examples of Trauma relieved as a prelude to healing and recovery

Here is a list of successful use of the Rewind trance method. The listing is just what came into my mind by a quick recall of past cases, written down in no particular order and in no way complete.

- Periods of abuse by an uncle and the subsequent trauma around the lack of family support
- Experiences of a very a difficult family gathering, dominated by rejection and loneliness
- Veteran of Basra, reliving a six week period of siege
- A car accident that led to a phobia of motorways….an accident on a roof that was still causing a fear of height, fifty years later….a hospital visit with mother that was generating a needle phobia fifteen years on
- The death of a much loved parent and the subsequent pressure of having to cope
- School bullying that extended to feeling of loneliness and separation and collapsing self confidence
- A teenage school humiliation involving the breaking of equipment
- Sickness on a tube journey late at night
- Mugging attack in the middle of the street in broad daylight
- The slow realisation that a grave career mistake had been made and that at the time, nothing could be done to rectify the mistake
- Extreme embarrassment at an office presentation
- Panic attacks extending over a month with the first particularly terrifying
- Memory of the awfulness of that first depression

- Discovery as a teenager that for many years previously her much loved father had been conducting a clandestine affair

k) Want to understand and relieve Depression – then focus on Emotions and not Thoughts?

Emotions not thoughts – it's that simple. And I confirm this to myself every day in my therapy room. If you can quieten down the emotional storm and then focus on using emotions well – i.e. to get that life working better, then healing will invariably happen.

This is my take on what Emotions are all about – of how Human Givens synthesises what is known.

Emotions are the fuel that drives action Having understood that human beings are living entities that spend their existence in taking action to get essential needs met, it is the emotion that flows and courses within us that is the energy that drives that action. You could say that without emotions, there would be no movement at all and we would not be alive.

Emotion as the expectation of action is how Joe Griffin (with Ivan Tyrell the founders of Human Givens) describes it or if you like, as the cranking up ready for action. The word emotion gives the game away. It is about motion and movement. So anger is the expectation that you will have to defend yourself, in response to a perceived threat and fear is the movement away from a threat. And the looking forward to a pleasure is the opening to relaxing and enjoying and disappointment is the gearing up to be evaluating and coping with something that is not working out and so on.

Emotions can also be understood as an information system that transmits signals to our action centres so we can respond to what we find in the environment – or as potentially subtle and sophisticated sensors that connects to our processing system that takes in what it needs to in order to make sense of what is happening out there.

Metaphorical pattern matching is the key mechanism by which this all works, which is central (though I hasten to add, not original) to the Human Givens approach.

We all understand the infinite variety of the world by seeing it as being 'like' something else and this 'like' is stored as a pattern in our unconscious memory bank. And as we make a connection with this pattern – an emotion will arise to communicate to us – intuitively if you like – so that we can make sense of it and if necessary act on it.

Pattern matching is the means by which we can make sense of what we find in our environment – by matching that up to what we have already processed and stored before. Pattern matching is always metaphorical as we will never have been able to exactly replicate what is now happening from our past experiences. What we have stored is "like" what is happening now.

The crucial aspect of pattern matching is that all matching is tagged by an emotion. And thoughts? Well they just tag along behind, like a faithful dog.

CHAPTER 23

AN INTRODUCTION TO HUMAN GIVENS

These edited down Depression Help blog posts are for all those who have not heard of Human Givens but are intrigued.... and those who have heard of Human Givens but know that they want to know more.

a) So what is Human Givens?

b) Human Givens Organising Idea: arrogant tosh or deep and profound?

c) The Human Givens explanation of what is "mental illness"

d) The Human Givens way to relief from "mental illness"

e) Human Givens explains why we dream…and so explains Depression

f) Healing from mental problems – it's all about the emotion

g) What does a Human Givens counsellor do that is so special?

h) Depression help is much more than a list of depression tips

i) A water hose out of control is a metaphor for the emotions that cause depression?

a) So what is Human Givens?

Human Givens has an explanation of how the brain manufactures depression. It is easy to understand and when understood, then help for depression is normally rapid and effective.

But what is Human Givens? Well it is not another model of therapy and neither has it a long pedigree. Yet already it is changing the way we understand and treat mental illnesses in the UK. It is also a great challenge to the conventional wisdom.

Beginnings The first seminars and workshops by Ivan Tyrell and Joe Griffin, the founders of the Human Givens approach were in the UK in the late 1990s. Ivan and Joe (now well into their retirement) are still the main teachers and drivers of the project

At the core of the HG approach is a very simple, easy to understand yet profound Organising Idea of what it is to be human. And to this has been added some original science (including a new theory of why we dream, from which depressions can be easily understood and treated) and a brilliantly expressed and delivered synthesis of what is the best of modern psychology and neuroscience. Depending on what you are looking for, from HG you can see a better way to undertake psychotherapy, a better way to run a company or a country and a more profound and deeper understanding of spirituality and what it is to be human.

The teaching of Human Givens is how Joe and Ivan have earned their livelihood. From all of this, Joe and

Ivan have created a teaching programme which is delivering a small number of really excellent counsellors and in addition a greater number of mainly public sector administrators and health professionals who know a little bit. Their programme and teaching is far superior and simpler to anything else out there (believe me) and so quite naturally there are now many vested interests who complain about HG's lack of evidence and arrogance. Notwithstanding there is already peer reviewed and hence academically acceptable evidence of its effectiveness and so HG is already beginning to get recognition within the NHS as a useful model of counselling/psychotherapy. Within 15 years of the first seminars – that is an amazing achievement. There is now also an impressive body of literature and websites – most of which are either written by Joe and Ivan or closely supervised by them.

What needs to be understood is that at its core and despite how it is seen in the public eye, Human Givens is not just another therapy model, like hundreds of others but something altogether more. With Human Givens there is a simple organising idea or paradigm together with key insights based on modern understanding of how the brain works which has applications to pretty well all areas of human activity – personal development, mental healing, public policy, corporate policy and indeed political philosophy and principles.

The tautological assumption is that since HG is based on what it is to be human, then all successful human activity will be based on the successful application of HG ideas and all human problems can be understood as coming from a failure to work with these. This would seem to be an unbelievably arrogant thing to say of course. It is not saying is that HG has to be at the centre of teaching, organisation and public policy but only that if these areas are working well, the HG ideas will be there even if unknowingly.

And I would say, having studied HG and worked with it professionally as a successful private practitioner for ten years now and for my personal development also and having read widely and been a close observer of the political scene, that Griffin and Tyrell's ideas are indeed profound and deep but also grounded and practical and actually do what I am saying is on the tin.

b) Human Givens Organising Idea: arrogant tosh or deep and profound?

I have argued that Human Givens is not just another model of counselling. It is much more ambitious than that, being no less than a new understanding of what it is to be human – that is rooted in science and common sense. Reading this, you the reader will probably have one of two reactions. One is to dismiss Human Givens as arrogant self-indulgent tosh. The other is to be excited and curious. Well I urge you to read what follows with an open mind and then see what you think – arrogant tosh or quite profound and deep?

The Organising Idea Human Givens are what we are born with, the templates for our species, Nature's endowment to each of us. These givens come in two kinds:

- The physical and emotional **needs** evolution has programmed into us, which seeks fulfilment through our interaction with the environment

- The **resources** (or tools) nature provided us with to help us get those needs met

And so, what we do every minute of the day (you could say) is to use our resources as best we can to try to get our essential emotional needs met.

Further, if needs are not well met, then emotional and mental difficulties will inevitably arise. A corollary is that mental and emotional problems will be impossible for anyone who is living a life of balance where resources are working well enough such that needs are reasonably or very well met. Think about it! Do you know anyone who is using their resources to get their needs met (i.e. leading a balanced life) but emotionally distressed? If you do, then that person needs to cherished and marvelled at – as a robin in midsummer or a four leaved clover. This organising idea is in many ways a statement of the "bleeding obvious" and no one to whom I have expressed it has ever come up with any significant reservation. Indeed the typical reaction is to nod automatically.

Notwithstanding, this organising idea if truly absorbed and understood does have profound consequences for both talking therapy and for understanding oneself and indeed society. This is because the idea keeps you grounded and asking the right questions. Where and in what way are needs not being met right now? What has changed to bring this about? And what needs to change for needs to be better met? So, rather than getting lost in metaphysical questions and introspections of the nature of what might be wrong or of absences and lacks that can lead you further into a morass of introspection, the focus shifts to problem solving, setting goals, looking for small practical steps in the right direction and crucially to a useful understanding of human psychology or human resources.

Essential Human NEEDS, according to Human Givens. Human Givens identifies nine emotional needs, all of which are explained as being equally important and all of which it is asserted must be well met for emotional health.

1. Security — feeling safe in an environment which allows you to develop fully
2. Attention (to give and receive it) — a form of nutrition
3. Sense of autonomy and control — having volition to make responsible choices
4. Being emotionally connected to others – friendship, intimacy — knowing that at least one other person accepts you totally for who you are, "warts 'n' all"
5. Feeling part of a wider community by having connections beyond your family and close friends
6. Privacy — opportunity to reflect and consolidate experience
7. Sense of status within social groupings
8. Sense of competence and achievement
9. Meaning and purpose — which come from being stretched in what we do and think

The RESOURCES nature has endowed us with to get essential needs met. Human Givens use a wonderfully evocative metaphor to explain the resources we have and the job they have evolved to do. They are our guidance system, pointing us toward what we must do to live a life that works (i.e. get our needs well met).

There are eight resources, by the HG formulation

1. Complex long term memory, to enable us to add to our innate knowledge and learn

2. The ability to build rapport, empathise and connect with others

3. Imagination, which enables us to focus our attention away from our emotions and so solve problems that get our needs met

4. Emotions and instincts

5. A conscious, rational mind that can question, analyse and plan

6. The ability to 'know' — that is, understand the world unconsciously through metaphorical pattern matching

7. An observing self — that part of us that can step back and be aware of itself as a unique centre of awareness

8. A dreaming brain that preserves the integrity of our emotional inheritance every night by metaphorically defusing expectations held in the autonomic arousal system because they were not acted out the previous day.

Understanding mental illness From this Organising Idea comes another profound truth that differentiates Human Givens from most other approaches to mental healing. It is that it leads to an understanding of what might be the source of mental difficulties or illnesses, as the psychiatric profession is wont to call them. The profession medicalises mental illness in a way that is nothing short of scandalous (or laughable). The HG organising idea in contrast allows one to move more confidently from the self-serving motivation and habits of the psychiatric profession and their good friends in the pharmaceutical, insurance and health industries – to seeing mental difficulties in an empowering and useful way. As I say, this is what is easy to do from a Human Givens perspective.

Human Givens understands mental problems as the consequence of failing attempts to live a life that works – in other words using resources effectively enough such that needs are met. For if despite our best efforts, life continues not to work, then we will look for solutions and/or ways of coping which can become desperate. And this desperation can make matters worse – so much so that the depressions, anxieties, obsessions, angers, addictive, obsessive and psychotic behaviours that then arise can be seen as indications of failure to get needs met, a failure that will be unravelling on certain predictable lines.

c) The Human Givens explanation of what is "mental illness"

Just imagine that a large part of the mental and emotional problems that people endure are not illnesses.

That rather than see these difficulties as indicators of a physical deficiency or lack or weakness in the brain or mind or wherever it might be, that they are instead indicators of what has happened to them and how they are coping with that at this moment. And that if they are in a bad way emotionally and mentally, it is not necessarily saying something fundamental and unchanging about their mental capacities but about how bad the past might have been and how well their resources and capacities are now serving them.

That all you see now is a snapshot but what you need to appreciate is that there is a movie there too – with moving parts and a story over time and the prospect of a future. And knowing this and having understood a smattering of Darwin you have grasped the idea that the consequence of all change depends on where you were before and how you got there and that vicious circles can develop for quite a time that take you further and further away from the best place to be. And that our natural capacities that can heal us quite naturally might need some help sometimes. Just imagine that.

And following on from the idea of change and evolution, you acknowledge that humans are living creatures that take in essential nutrition in order to grow and evolve and that without this nutrition they would fade and die. And that nutrition is much more than food and water and includes nutrition for our mind and emotions. That we need to feel safe, to have control and so be able to take decisions that enhance our relationships and sense of community and our sense of meaning and the satisfaction we can get from the work we do. And indeed as living creatures, we need to be active and be able to take decisions and then act upon them.

If these ideas seems pretty unexceptional, then it is not a very big step to appreciate that if for whatever reason, some or all of this essential mind nutrition is absent or not flowing in sufficient quantities, then that ain't good. And that maybe we might feel stressed and this might transform into all kinds of things – depressions, anxieties, addictions and who knows what else. And if this in turn meant we were less able to get our essential mind nutrition, then our emotional and mental state might really begin to look pretty bad. Such that some very ignorant people might even say we were mentally ill.

What might the reasons be that push us down into such a vicious circle? Well it could be our circumstances or life experiences – of loss, hurt, pain and deprivation. After all, for all of us there are limits to what we can healthily endure. And second, we may have developed ways of coping with past hurts and suffering that are not now helping but nevertheless we just seem to repeat them over and over despite how hard we try to stop. In particular many of us will have experienced events (short or long enduring) that stay as trauma or threshold trauma and the emotion around the memory of these will bubble up periodically or even continuously and when that happens we have no good way to deal with it. And what if this means that our natural resources or guidance system that ideally should direct us to the necessary action that leads to a life where our emotional needs are being well fed is doing no such thing? I think the answer to that is pretty obvious!

What I have described here is the best way I know to convey the principles behind the Human Givens organising idea.

So ponder this. If this explanation of what might be happening for those who believe and are diagnosed as mentally ill is close to the truth – then we would not need to bother with spurious and wasteful talk of mental health stigma. Would we?

d) The Human Givens way to relief from "mental illness"

I have teased out some of the main ideas of Human Givens as they explain what most mental problems might be about. And I have also suggested that there is a social dimension (to put it mildly) to causing mental problems in the UK today. That our society may not be conducive to the large majority of us getting our essential emotional nutrition (to use HG speak). Now, if there is anything in what I am saying, then the NHS and the psychiatry profession is not where we will find many answers and solutions.

So what are the principles that should guide an individual in emotional distress or someone trying to help that person?

What is needed firstly, is to facilitate movement and change and to overcome any quite natural resistance. It is to shift attention towards solutions and more empowering interpretations of the present and away from a focus on what is wrong. Resources need to be healed and notably trauma must be cleared. And finally action encouraged, motivation built and goals set that gets essential emotional needs better met.

That (in my nutshell) is what Human Givens healing is about and it should be clear that the existence or otherwise of mental health stigma, real or imagined need play no part at all. But if this HG approach is anywhere near the truth but you find your way to a system that sees your situation as an illness that requires doctors and drugs to fix, then it is hardly surprisingly that you search for explanations, however farfetched or unhelpful. And the existence of stigma could seem to fit the bill. But it is not stigma that you dealing with but ignorance, pure and simple.

e) Human Givens explains why we dream…and so explains Depression

The Human Givens hypothesis of what dreaming is for and why it plays such an essential role in supporting healthy emotions is the one clearly original contribution by Human Givens (notably Joe Griffin) to modern psychological understanding and from this to the understanding of what depression and psychosis is all about.

Here I am summarising the ideas as best I can, sometimes using Griffin's own words.

Human Givens explains dreaming An emotion, can be understood as an expectation or a physical preparing for action. For example, a worry is an emotion felt in your body that is expecting action on your part to clear away a potential problem in the future.

When the emotion is not acted upon it then stays in the body uncompleted. And what dreaming does every night is to discharge that uncompleted emotion – by playing it out in metaphor. Dreaming is the emotional flush toilet or the essential nightly maintenance that frees our emotions to serve us effectively the next day.

Griffin's insight was to realise that dreams act out our unexpressed emotional expectations (positive and negative) through the medium of metaphor. They are imaginary, metaphorical and perceptual experiences that occur primarily in REM sleep and they have the effect of preserving the integrity of our emotional responses.

Griffin's research showed that all dreams are expressed in the form of sensory metaphors. The reason for this is found in the biology of dreaming and the REM state itself, which is the experience of all mammals. Thus for example, we know that instinctive behaviours are programmed during the REM state in the foetus and the neonate and Griffin could then postulate that the REM state is the state that humans access in order to imagine, remember and learn. Griffin then theorises that the REM state will not just occur when dreaming but is also accessed as the trance state when learning or when attempting to remember or focussing on just one thing.

Griffin called his dreaming theory **the expectation fulfilment theory of dreams**. In summary, the essential points to understand about dreaming, which is the deepest trance state we enter are:

- Dreams are metaphorical translations of waking expectations

- Expectations which cause emotional arousal that is not acted upon during the day are the basis of dreams during sleep that night
- Dreaming then deactivates that emotional arousal by completing the expectation pattern metaphorically, freeing the brain to respond afresh to each new day

The clincher – dreams can explains depression and perhaps psychosis It has been known for years that depression has something to do with sleep. For example, experiments had shown quite clearly that if you deprive depressed people of sleep, then the depression lessened. However, it was not until Joe Griffin undertook his ground breaking research into why we dream, that it became clear what a depression is and how it can be lifted.

Human Givens postulates that depression is a response to excessive ruminations and arousals, caused by a life which is not working. This then requires a large amount of REM dreaming while sleeping in an attempt to deactivate these arousals. But dreaming takes a lot of energy and the brain becomes too exhausted to complete the required dreaming and so the person wakes up in a state of exhaustion and de-motivation. A downward spiral begins – of worry, exhausting sleep, de-motivation and a growing incapacity to act effectively to get the initial problem solved and so get needs better met.

How might psychosis fit in? The idea is as follows – that when stress levels get very high, especially for individuals with vivid imaginative resources, the dream state begins to leak into the wakened state. Then the boundaries between the sleeping REM and the awaked REM states blur such that individuals experience waking dreams. There is then no distinction between the realities that are processed from ones senses (waking reality) and dreaming, which as we know is closed off from external senses and where the extraordinary and bizarre can be easily accepted. Could this be an explanation of the psychotic or schizophrenic state?

f) Healing from mental problems – it's all about the emotion

It is axiomatic that for those in mental distress, emotional arousal will be high (periodically or continually) and that it is the reaction to this whirlpool of emotion that is an integral part of mental distress. Or to put it another way, high emotional arousal makes us all stupid and so unable to act and think well – and if we are unable to act and think well, then mental problems will follow (as night follows day). The corollary is also true – that a productive use of subtle emotional clues and hence useful learning and action will only take place when calm and then we are emotionally healthy.

Human Givens argues that for all of us, emotions will precede and drive the thought and action. It follows that therapies which focus on challenging the thought (such as cognitive behavioural therapy or CBT) will always be flawed or at best hard work.

Finally if the shifting of and the working with emotions is the essence of effective therapy, then the use of trance tools and methods would seem pretty important – as this is the route into the REM state which is where emotions can be accessed and moderated. Is it too obvious to remark that for talking therapies that do not use trance (such as CBT), it is like asking GPs to treat bacterial infection without antibiotics or plumbers to mend central heating systems without screwdrivers?

So, if the core of mental distress is the failure of emotional resources to be working well; it will be with emotions that healing begins. A classic question asked by a Human Givens therapist would therefore be: "What are the emotions saying and how well or badly are they being used in support of the necessary action that will cause essential emotional needs to be better met?" And then a second question – "what can I do that will allow emotional resources to be working more effectively and so better support action and change that get needs better met?"

g) What does a Human Givens counsellor do that is so special?

Human Givens is a slightly odd name for something which makes so much sense, that when you understand the basics of it, it is hard to imagine why everybody does not see things that way. And you can certainly understand why Human Givens counsellors are so effective.

This is a summary of how we see things and how we go about helping people lost in depression, anxieties, addictions, overwhelming life problems and so on.

1) We want to know how well that person's life is working now. Specifically what essential human needs are not being met – around safety, control, relationships

and the work they do. We ask this because we know that if a person's needs are being well met, then they will be OK.

2) We then want to understand how that person got where there are now? What happened to them, both recently or further back that meant that they found they could not cope, however hard they tried and then things got worse and not better.

3) We would then want begin to heal some of that person's resources, particularly focusing on their emotions. Because we would see clearly that their emotions were often out of control and as a result, self-confidence was low. And we know how to do this in most cases – often by using hypnotherapy and trance and being able to clear away traumatic memories.

4) Finally we will help our client refocus on doing things so that they can take the necessary action to get their life working better. We would remind them of their strengths and good experiences, that maybe they had forgotten about.

h) Depression help is much more than a list of depression tips

If you were teaching chess to a complete beginner you would not start by teaching the rules governing how each of the chess pieces move – the pawn, the bishop, the castle and so on. No – you would state what was the objective of the game – namely to checkmate the opposing king. Yes, you need to teach the moves early on and it would be very important that a chess beginner had fully mastered them. But the mastering of the moves comes second to knowing what is actually going on in the game. And of course (and this is a really important point) that to know what is the purpose of the game will then make the learning of the moves much easier.

So it is with depression. There is a mountain of information and sources that makes pretty sensible points about what might help to relieve a depression. But if you have no idea about what actually is the real cause of these awful depression experiences and why they seem to be getting worse whatever you do – well all of these tips and ideas will fall well short of what is needed.

What are the tips that you will find in pretty well every depression help source? Let's start with regular exercise and the eating of nutritious food and the cutting down of sugars and heavily processed food. There is no doubt that these are no bad things. And the more depressed people find that they can focus on simple tasks or manage to get out in the community even if it is the last thing they want to do – then this can be pretty helpful too. And there are many websites that will be saying this and I for one would never argue against any of it. Laughing is good too and meditation (very popular advice, at least right now) and (my favourite) – the cultivation of a practice of daily gratitude.

These are all good but on their own they are just not enough. Like Hungarian goulash without the paprika – something is missing.

And what is it that is missing? It is a clear explanation and understanding of what a depression is – namely the exhaustion caused by worrying too much and hence engaging in far too much high energy dreaming.

And when you know it AND really know it – why then everything else makes much more sense and you will be knowing why you are doing what everyone says you should do. And you will know more than most of them, including the experts (so called).

i) A water hose out of control is a metaphor for the emotions that cause depression?

Imagine a garden hose in full flow. It looks fun – squirting out and soaking everybody and everything that might get in its way. The reason I choose this particular hose image was because of the hands squeezing the head of the hose are perhaps trying and failing to usefully control the water flow and because it is quite easy to see the power of the jet. It is fun to play with hoses like this but you can never use them seriously if the flow is so strong.

Is this a little like emotions?

Just as the water flow through a hose has to be the right pressure and not too powerful, so the same is true of emotions if they are to be useful and not destructive. When emotions are very strong whether it is anger or fear or in the case of most depressions, an overwhelming hopelessness that induces a terrifying fearfulness, then they are of no possible use and indeed will do serious damage.

But remember that emotions that are flowing at the

right pressure so that they can be directed usefully toward where they are needed are in fact doing the job that they are intended to do. Emotions drive action and movement and so are essential to human life. Without emotions, humanity would be motionless.

And that is why the overwhelming objective of my work with depressed clients is to help them use their emotions well and to be in control of them. That they are using their emotions productively to get a life that works for them or in Human Givens parlance, to get their essential emotional needs met.

Which is why trance is such a powerful tool – for in a trance state, emotions can easily be touched and redirected. And to understand that in depression, dreaming cannot do its essential job properly – of emotional maintenance.

CHAPTER 24

HOME TRUTHS ABOUT DEPRESSION HELP ON THE NHS

Read these edited down blog post and perhaps you will be as angry and despairing as I am – as I contemplate the terrible mess we are in – relying on the NHS (of all people) to relieve our depression epidemic.

a) Depression help and why the NHS is not up to the task?

b) If depression is not a mental illness – where does that leave the NHS?

c) Why is CBT now the only NHS talking therapy for depression – when it is not up to it?

d) A peashooter to kill an elephant – why CBT is not the answer for depression relief

e) The truth about anti-depressants – they don't do what they say on the tin

f) Antidepressants or CBT for depression: about as useful a choice as a Big Mac or KFC

g) Putting it together – Depression, the NHS, Cognitive Behavioural Therapy and all that jazz

a) Depression help and why the NHS is not up to the task?

We all know the scorpion and frog story.

"A scorpion and a frog meet on the bank of a stream and the scorpion asks the frog to carry him across on its back. The frog asks, "How do I know you won't sting me?" The scorpion says, "Because if I do, I will die too."

The frog is satisfied, and they set out, but in midstream, the scorpion stings the frog. The frog feels the onset of paralysis and starts to sink, knowing they both will drown, but has just enough time to gasp "Why?"

Replies the scorpion: "It's my nature…"

This story speaks a big truth that we all have to understand and work with every day. You can only ask something of a person or an organisation and then expect it to be delivered if they are capable of delivering it. If it is in their nature.

So consider the nature of the NHS. It is set up to deliver medical methods and procedures that can be rolled out nationwide. And for hip replacements and emergency stroke treatment and much else, the NHS can deliver. Like McDonald's hamburgers, the same medical treatment will, broadly speaking, be in Inverness as in Doncaster as in Cornwall as anywhere.

But what if the delivery of depression counselling can never be standardised? What if there is no single counselling approach that is better than other? And horror of horrors, some counsellors are better than others. And that these good counsellors need to be allowed to get on and do their stuff

The answer is that the NHS cannot cope with that – because it goes against its nature. The nature of the NHS is to medicalise and to standardise – so to roll out nationwide. But the best counselling cannot be standardised. We know that. The evidence is beyond doubt and indeed there will be people employed by the NHS who will also know it too. But they will not be able to speak it and be heard.

And so the NHS tries and tries to standardise and to medicalise because that is what it does.

The current attempt by the NHS to standardise counselling has been to elevate Cognitive Behavioural Therapy (CBT) above all the rest. They have found spurious evidence that it is the best and now there is a CBT industry that can earn a nice living by delivering this standardised and manualised treatment nationwide and who will tenaciously protect the NHS provision of CBT from all comers. Soon one feels that monkeys will be able to do it. But CBT will never deliver what is being promised because counselling cannot be standardised. Notwithstanding, the NHS will keep going – as ever in thrall to the vested interests of the deliverers of standardisation as it knows no other way. It is its nature, like the scorpion.

b) If depression is not a mental illness – where does that leave the NHS

Back to the scorpion

You cannot expect a person or institution to go against its nature. If you do, then you will only have yourself to blame when it all goes wrong. The scorpion metaphor works well to explain the problems the NHS has in setting up a nationwide counselling service for depression relief. If the nature of counselling is that it cannot be standardised and rolled out nationwide, then the NHS cannot do it. It is against its nature.

But there is more.

What if there was no medical test for depression, like there is for diabetes or high blood pressure? What if the only explanation that can credibly explain the apparent rise of depression to (we are told) epidemic levels over the past fifty years or so, is to understand the impact of our rapidly changing society? What if you accepted what Human Givens says about the causes of depression for an individual – that it is about ruminating and dreaming too much and that such an explanation fits easily into a social explanation for an increased nationwide incidence of depression?

How would the NHS cope with depression if this is how it is?

The answer is not well at all – because again, the NHS would be going against its nature. The NHS is designed to deal with the nation's physical health – to fix our bodies, to keep the pain under control and to administer tests, medication and procedures, by medically trained personnel – all of which have been passed according to conventional scientific principles.

So why are we surprised that the NHS makes such a mess of depression relief and that the epidemic keeps growing? We are asking the NHS to deal with the consequences of the nation's social problems – the stress of modern life, the breakdown of family and community, the increasing dependence on the state…and so on.

Why is the NHS the dumping ground, by politicians but also the general public to solve social problems that are way beyond its competence? We have serious social issues around obesity, social care for the elderly and an apparent epidemic of mental problems – notably depression, but also addictions and anxieties. Who among us can honestly say, hand on heart, that these problems are medical and to be sorted out by the NHS?

Against its nature – for sure

c) Why is CBT now the only NHS talking therapy for depression – when it is not up to

Cognitive behavioural therapy is fundamentally flawed. The argument goes like this. If emotions come before thoughts and as CBT works by challenging thoughts, why would you ever think that CBT would ever be much help in clearing depression – about as useful as a peashooter to down an elephant maybe? That was a bit rude, but you get the idea.

So why does your GP only offer CBT along with antidepressants for depression relief when it is so theoretically weak? The answer is of course because the NHS has concluded (and not your GP) that CBT is the one for them. They will say that this is because it is proven to be the best – but that is just not so (or to be precise not relevant). No, CBT is now the main talking therapy available from the NHS for depression relief because of institutional and bureaucratic ignorance and now increasingly powerful vested interests.

There are two truths that apply to all talking therapy, including CBT. These truths are that there is no model of therapy better than any other but some therapists are better than others. This is a conclusion, though unambiguously proven cannot be accepted by the NHS. Like the scorpion, it goes against the nature of the NHS to accept the implication of these truths. For if it did accept them, then the NHS could not even pretend to be able to develop a therapy approach that it could standardise and be able to roll out across the nation, like Tesco or BP.

So we are lumbered with CBT and as the CBT interests become ever more powerful, there is probably nothing that we can do about it – for at least as long as we expect the NHS to clear up our depression epidemic.

I am not saying that CBT does not help depressed people or more accurately that some therapists trained in CBT (and who knows what they actually do in the therapy room) do not do a good job. It is the bureaucracy and vested interests and the limited choice that is the problem (or part of it).

d) A peashooter to kill an elephant – why CBT is not the answer for depression relief

This posting is bitching about cognitive behavioural therapy or CBT. Obviously there is envy and jealousy lurking around. CBT is everywhere now in the NHS (and in the US too) – the favoured psychological treatment for depression. And why might this be? Well, it ain't because it is the best or even much good. And if you don't believe me, read what Amanda of Ohio says.

"I did cognitive behavioural therapy it had limited success as it worked for awhile, however I found myself so tense all the time from having to evaluate every single thought I had 24 hours a day every day. Eventually my defences would wear down and I would relax and then I would slip right back into depression again. It was defeating and killed my hope. They never understood was once that feeling stabbed me I was done for and my ability to think clearly rationally disappeared so CBT couldn't help me then, before sure after the switch never."

This posting is attempting to keep an elevated tone by talking of psychological theory and why CBT is based on false and inadequate understanding of how the brain works. But in attempting to keep the tone up, I am not writing an academic blog. I am simply repeating what I have learnt from my Human Givens training IF and it is a big IF – it has been confirmed as right by my work with clients.

So I know that emotions come before thoughts. As far as I am concerned it is not for debate – it's a no brainer. It is obviously true for a powerful trauma which is normally driven by an overwhelming emotion of fear. That clearly comes ahead of a thought such as "shit this is dangerous, maybe I should run away" But I know that it applies to much subtler emotions as well – of feelings of unease, of anticipation or confusion. The emotion will arise as a pattern match and that from this a thought will arise, to give it shape and meaning – to mark it if you like.

So if this is the case, why would you take CBT seriously? CBT is about challenging thoughts. It is about changing how you think. It is about breaking down complex thoughts and behaviours that are keeping you stuck. It is about facing up to clearly unhelpful black and white thoughts such as – "I am stupid and people hate me" and "I cannot do anything about this and for the rest of my life, I am doomed" and so on.

But feelings come first. Especially feelings of exhaustion and the terror of not knowing why you are feeling so bad and bewildered because you have no idea why you are lost in a vicious circle of tiredness and useless rumination.

In these circumstances and knowing that, why would you think for minute that someone trained in CBT would have any idea at all what to do for you? Well maybe a tiny bit – but be no more useful than a peashooter attempting to down an elephant.

e) The truth about anti-depressants – they don't do what they say on the tin

If you go to your GP depressed and mentally exhausted the chances are that you will be offered antidepressants of some kind. And the assumption is that this is an effective and proven treatment. Not so.

The Human Givens institute summarises as positively as it can what the evidence on anti-depressants says.

"Anti-depressants work in aggregate about as well as placebo which means about one third of people benefit. But of course they do not pretend to treat the root cause and so there is a high rate of relapse. And a quarter of users will do less well than placebo."

And there are side effects – from an increased suicide risk, loss of sex drive, dizziness, nausea, fatigue, headaches and so on Finally, a third of those taking anti-depressants will suffer withdrawal symptoms."

So not that impressive! And if you ask for GPs private views on anti-depressants, then they are not that impressed either.

Now, read the summary of Charles O'Connell's devastating critique of medication for mental illness in general and anti-depressants in particular (in the 2011 Human Givens Journal).

"When all the data of all is found and used, the efficacy of drugs in the field of mental health is invariably shown to be insignificant. The pharmaceutical companies play on our ignorance and fear and the supply monopoly and high regulation of health services to cream us"

More from Mr O'Connell:

- *Big Pharma controls all of the trials pertaining to their drugs and have total control of the information generated by these trials.*

- *Data is distorted in a number of ways – e.g. only one trial needs to show results better than placebo – there can be 20 failures which will be hidden.*

- *There are biases over the length of the study comparisons – which can always be manipulated in favour of the new drug.*

- *The companies control the publication of clinical trials and have sole ownership of the data. It can therefore simply choose not to publish results unfavourable to the drug and if the results of the trial appear favourable, then drug companies will frequently publish the data in multiple publications taking slightly different angles in each paper and so having the effect of increasing the profile of the drug and making it appear more favourable than in fact it is.*

- *The doctors cannot be trusted. Despite the tighter regulation, pharmaceutical companies are nothing if not extremely effective as marketing machines and the minor inconvenience of not being able to woo local doctors through their stomachs has not dented its influence. There will still be all-expenses-paid trips to exotic locations to present the findings of the trial of meetings that are often held solely for the purpose of launching the drug.*

- *The medical industry has also expanded the definition of illness and created a range of conditions in the treatment of which the drug companies can sell their wares. The usual practice is to select an established condition, find certain features of it that had appeared to a much lesser extent in normal people and imply that the disorder is a continuum from mild to severe.*

- *Non-illnesses created in this manner include male pattern baldness, short stature, erectile dysfunction, menopause, depression, attention deficit hyperactivity disorder and shyness.*

- *In the area of mental health a huge range of conditions such as complex somatic symptoms disorder, separation anxiety disorder and schizotypal personality disorder has been invented to facilitate the sale of drugs to treat them.*

Antidepressants don't work

Mood in humans is regulated by a myriad of systems in the body including the neurotransmitters serotonin, noradrenalin, dopamine, glutamate gamma amino butyric acid (GABA) and endorphins. These neurotransmitters have multiple functions in the body and interact with many different receptors. For serotonin alone, there are at least 13 receptor subtypes in the body at which serotonin exerts its effect.

There is much evidence that these various systems interact, serving to maintain a healthy balance by complex regulatory and compensatory relationships, as the brain is a plastic malleable organ, the natural dominance or recessive nurse of any of these systems can also be modulated through learned behaviour.

Despite this knowledge, the thrust of chemical treatment of low mood, sponsored by pharmaceutical companies with their compliant allies in the medical industry, has mainly been towards interacting with a single transmitter system, such as serotonin. The issue of efficacy of antidepressants was raised many years ago. Earlier studies from the 1980s and 1990s tended to suggest that impressed depressants were 20 to 30% more effective than placebo. More recently, meta-analysis showed no differences at around 10 percent in recent meta-analysis – including all studies, published and unpublished (in other words including those hidden by the pharmaceutical industry). For antidepressants, the efficacy reached clinical significance only involving the most extremely depressed patients. And that this pattern is due to the increase in response to placebo rather than an increase in the response to medication.

When unpublished data are included, antidepressant efficacy comes strongly into question.

Another curiosity to these drugs that are advocated to clearly target the condition depression is the fact that manufacturers frequently expand the range of indications from the drug to increase the number of potential clients. The range can include such conditions as bulimia, OCD, generalised anxiety disorder, social phobia, panic disorder and post-dramatic stress disorder.

Overall, antidepressants have not been shown to substantially improve the plight of patients with low mood and are associated with many unpleasant and potentially harmful side-effects. It is little wonder that SSRIs have spectacularly failed to treat a condition for which they are marketed, but it is still extraordinary that antidepressants are the eighth most prescribed drug in the world with sales of $19 billion in 2009.
    Charles O'Connell – Human Givens Journal 2011

f) Antidepressants or CBT for depression: about as useful a choice as a Big Mac or KFC

You are starving and desperate for some decent food. And so you go to the only restaurant around – not that you are worried as the restaurant has a good reputation for knowing about good food and how to prepare it. And what does the menu offer? It has just two items – a Big Mac and KFC (Kentucky Fried chicken). That was it – no discussion. Take it or leave it – eat rubbish or starve.

We will each have our own reasons why such a choice would be less than appetising. Perhaps it is the knowledge of the large amount of homogenised and saturated fats, or the high salt content and crude flavouring or perhaps the absence of lightly cooked vegetables or subtle flavouring. But we would know, from what we have read and from earlier experiences of Big Macs and KFCs that we would want to do a lot better for our healthy nutritious meal. And we would be appalled at the restaurant – who exactly did they think they were kidding?

Well go to a GP looking for depression relief and you will be offered a menu of two items – CBT (cognitive behavioural therapy) or antidepressants. And taken together they are about as satisfactory and acceptable as a choice between a Big Mac and KFC.

We know that neither is what they seem to be - the lack of evidence supporting antidepressants and how powerful vested interests hide this. And what of CBT – is that any better? What the evidence says very clearly is that CBT is no better than any other talking therapy and anyway, it is not the therapy model that is important, but the therapist.

So there you have it – CBT or antidepressants, a Big Mac or a KFC. Neither will help you reliably with your depression nor be much good feeding you healthily.

g) Putting it together – Depression, the NHS, Cognitive Behavioural Therapy and all that jazz

The NHS is not set up to cure depression

- Depression is not an illness
- The NHS cannot "cure" the social ills of society
- There are good therapists and bad therapists and this has nothing to do with what their model of therapy is? So how can the NHS ever be able to set up a standard depression treatment that will be the same everywhere
- Treating depression is not like replacing hips or inoculating against measles

The NHS is set up to fix bodies and not minds

- The NHS mind-set is medical – that if you search long enough and apply sound scientific methods then physical disabilities can be explained and once understood, can in principle be cured or ameliorated – by a judicious combination of medication, physical intervention and other physical applications.
- So why is the NHS the dumping ground, by politicians but also the general public to solve social problems that are way beyond its competence?
- We have serious social issues around obesity, social

care for the elderly and an apparent epidemic of mental problems – notably depression, but also addictions and anxieties. Who amongst us can honestly say, hand on heart, that these problems are medical?

What if depression is not a medical condition, but psychological?

- Since the war, the incidence of depression has exploded from being very rare to affecting we are repeatedly told, 1 in 4 of the population during their life time. How can depression be physical– the human body does not change that quickly.

- The explanation of depression here is based on the Human Givens. This says that a depression is a normal and indeed healthy response to extreme stress and worry. It is not an illness. And based on that principle, there is now hard evidence that Human Givens trained therapists can help the large majority of the clients they see with depression.

- Over the past fifty years we have seen family breakdown, rising materialism, the fracturing of community and work and the widespread delegation of responsibility to the state, to cure our social ills. Surely it is to this that we must look to explain our depression epidemic.

Your GP will tell you that your depression should be treated by a combination of medication and cognitive behavioural therapy (CBT)

What your GP will not tell you (and indeed may not know) is that the "evidence" that supports these recommendations for treatment is not credible and indeed is sinister and suspicious given the vested interests (e.g. pharmaceutical companies, the psychiatry profession).

GPs are in fact lukewarm in their attitude to anti-depressants. 71% believe them to be 'quite effective' but 57% say they are over-prescribed (Mental Health Foundation).

There are no silver bullets, active ingredients, no formulas or procedures that can be proved to assist recovery from depression.

Even after 100 years of trying there is not one (that's right not one) biological or chemical test for a single mental illness, including depression.

CHAPTER 25

MY CLIENT'S EXPERIENCES OF DEPRESSION RECOVERY

These client stories will give a flavour of how depression recovery can work in practice.

a) Drowning I: Isobel on the verge of extinction

b) Drowning II: Rachel on the verge of extinction

c) Nita and Rita needed just one word to reset – but which one was it?

d) The case of Mike – needing to create a new model for living, now he had retired

e) Barbara and Ros – attempting to reset in mid-stream

f) Harold and his diagnosis of Dysthymia

g) Fiona's recovery from Depression and a family campaign of ignorance and stigma

h) How often do NHS psychiatrists get it as badly wrong as for Norman?

i) How Depression can creep up quietly – but then can be dealt with

j) Carol's remarkable story – at last fighting free from a lifetime of depression

k) Clear Trauma and Depression can just melt away – the experience of two women

l) Peeling away the layers of an Onion – the case study of Tricia

m) When fear of depression is the problem – Trevor's experience

a) Drowning I: Isobel on the verge of extinction

Isobel (not her real name), single and in her late twenties came to see me in early December. What was noteworthy about Isobel was the depth of her depression (as measured by the CORE system I use) and that there was no obvious trigger cause or trauma to be dealt with. The truth was she believed (with good reason) that she was a capable young woman but had been so shocked by her descent into a trapped hell of emotions out of control and failure to get out on her own, that she was experiencing a raw terror and fear that was completely beyond her expectations or experience. Indeed in Isobel's case there remained a veneer of assurance about her – which belied her desperation. Her CORE score at that first session was 38 – the highest by far that I have ever come across (in over six years of using this measure) and much higher than I was expecting. Let me explain.

I ask all my clients at every session of therapy to complete a CORE 10 form, which measures their emotional health over the previous week – that I have come to trust to be reliable. There are ten questions, and each is scored from zero to four, depending on the distress indicated by each question (not at all, occasional, sometimes, all the time). The maximum theoretical score is therefore 40 (10 times 4) which would be an indicator of permanent distress, covering experiences of panic, anxiety, isolation, bad sleep, suicidal thoughts and so on. A score approaching 30 is quite rare in my experience and indicates severe distress, while any score over 25 is a red alert. Before Isobel, the highest score I had come across was 34 and I had found that scores at that level or slightly less related to clients enduring addictions.

To score 38 was almost beyond my belief and when I saw Isabel's score, it frightened me a little. She talked of suicide in a matter of fact way – knowing exactly how she would do it and finding each day was a big effort not to. But she had got nowhere from her GP, was taking antidepressants that were self-evidently doing her no good and I believed that I was her last best hope.

As is normal at a first session with a depressed client I only spent a little time asking Isobel about herself. I ascertained though that her waking up time in the morning was agonising for her but that she had just moved into shared accommodation where for the first time for a long time she felt it might be good for her. She also revealed in passing that she was a dress designer and gave a hint that she might be talented and that she revelled in her creativity. The other thing I got then was her determination to stand on her own feet and her ambition – now horribly thwarted for three years.

And then I normalised like mad – with the objective that she should begin to understand her situation less catastrophically and personally and so begin to worry less and get some energy back by dreaming less. I also emphasised that we would leave her problems to one side until she was feeling better. I urged her to listen to my Depression Mp3.

Isabel came back a week later and her CORE score had fallen to 24 – still high but a big improvement over the week. Isabel had noticed the improvement and was much more engaged in what I was saying. At that second session, we focused on job application efforts she felt she could make in the rag trade. An opening had come up, in selling and she felt she could do it and wanted it. We undertook an extended trance session which focused on her ability to put the nightmare of the last few years or so behind her. A week after that she returned, having applied for and had an interview, which she felt had gone well. Her CORE score had come down to 16 – indicating just moderate stress and an almost miraculous change in just two weeks. She emailed me a couple of days after that third session to say she had got the job and remarked that even a month before, there was no way she could even have contemplated applying.

At our final session, a fortnight later she was flying. She scored nine – an indicator of solid emotional health. And at that session I de-traumatised some remaining residual fears around the horror of her depression returning. She emailed me the next day to say that she felt that I had literally saved her life. And perhaps the truth is that I had.

b) Drowning II: Rachel on the verge of extinction

I have recounted Isobel's miraculous recovery from near extinction. At around the same time (towards the end of 2013) Rachel also came to see me and in some ways her depression experience and current situation had parallels with Isobel. The main similarity that struck me was that Rachel also saw herself as a capable person (as indeed she was) – and so "depressions did not happen to her". And then when it apparently did, the shock was even greater.

For Rachel, there had been medical problems concerning her shoulder that the NHS just could not seem to deal with. And this was allied to chronic problems around her main relationship and at work. She was a very committed social worker yet the defensiveness and politicisation of the job created addition pressures, while at the same time denying her the opportunity for real job satisfaction.

As far as was possible Rachel was taking things into her own hands. She had gone private in dealing with her shoulder and she was seeing me, having given up on the NHS and despite very unwillingly, continuing with medication. And she had taken leave of absence from work. To do such a thing however can be a mixed blessing as it encourages time for rumination and worry – and this was what was happening to Rachel. Additionally there were some emotional memories around a previous period of medical emergency that were exacerbating emotional arousal and feelings of being out of control.

Rachel took longer to recover than Isobel – a matter of a couple of months. I believe that this was because there were aspects to her life that did need to be changed and in theory she should not even begin this until her sleeping and dreaming were improving. In practice of course it is never as cut and dried as that and quite early on we both were thinking about how she might change her situation – notably to get greater job satisfaction.

And so Rachel began to recover. It was not one thing, but an accumulation of things. We worked on her becoming less fearful of being on her own (as her partner faded from the scene). She began to explore changing her work and maybe even going it alone in some form – and so as her sleep improved, a virtuous circle began to get underway. It took more than a couple of months before she had tuned her emotions around – she was sleeping well and getting her life sorted.

c) Nita and Rita needed just one word to reset – but which one was it?

Nita and Rita both came to see me a number of years ago now. Neither was highly depressed but chronically so. They were both worrying too much and for too long about an issue in their lives that they felt needed to be addressed. This worrying was unproductive as the issue was not being resolved. The consequence for both was that they were dreaming too much and so feeling less and less themselves. And this was unexpected as they saw themselves as capable individuals who dealt with such problems easily and by themselves.

For Nita the issue revolved around her relationship with her husband and how her career would fit in with his as he was an investment banker on his way to a prestigious position in New York. Rita's issue was also work related. She had a middle ranking clinical position in the NHS. Her problem was not that she felt what she did was not important (exactly the opposite), but that the combination of family pressures at home and nightmare bureaucratic restrictions at work meant that she felt permanently unfulfilled and so undecided about her future.

The Depression Optimist

For both Nita and Rita, my approach was not my typical one. That is to focus on the causes of depression (normalisation) and so shift attention temporarily away from rumination until dreaming and sleep improve and mental exhaustion recedes. Instead what I felt was needed was a reframe – a different interpretation for where Nita and Rita each found themselves, from which they themselves could begin to move.

And in both cases they subsequently told me, it was little more than a well-chosen word by me that did the trick. For Nita it was a reminder of previous times where she had managed to think outside the box. And for Rita it related to the opportunities that she knew were there at work that would be under her control – where she could focus much more on her satisfaction from one on one interaction with patients.

In fact, I could barely remember what I had said. I imagined that my approach was much more scatter-gun than they were implying (which is often the way), from which they had taken what they needed. In each case I was pretty certain that the breakthrough had come during a trance session and that I had used a metaphor that they could instinctively understand and use. Looking back after these years, I wonder what the metaphor might have been?

Mountain tops to see the bigger pictures, opening doors to many paths, a broad and deep river denoting all the many possibilities open to us all, a tide receding leaving behind what was really valuable...... I wonder what it was?

d) The case of Mike – needing to create a new model for living, now he had retired

Mike came to me chronically depressed, having been slowly sinking over the three or four years, since his retirement. He was in his early sixties and had a successful corporate career – beginning as an engineer but involving at an increasingly senior level, in overseas operations for a well-known US multinational.

His career had been hard work and insecure at times but ultimately rewarding – as he enjoyed much of it and he managed to provide substantial security and opportunity for his family. This had always been his major objective. As a result, he would say that his natural caution and predisposition to work hard and to plan carefully had been justified. And this was despite a difficult and fractious time at retirement when he felt that he had not been treated very well, particularly financially.

This caution and care had very much stayed with him in his retirement. It was as if he could not relax and let go – for his retirement seemed to bring ever more problems around his living circumstances and the management and uncertainty of his financial resources. A classic depression resulted, in terms of increasingly disturbed sleeping patterns, worrying and mental exhaustion – that seemed impossible to resolve as he "normally" would have done.

What emerged when helping Mike, was that he needed to work out a very different way to see the world and how he could best live in it. The old corporate model no longer worked.

And this became our main focus once we had relieved some of the exhaustion. He listened carefully and regularly to my Lift depression MP3 and we did some good relaxation trance work, notably around the period just before and after his retirement.

And then we conducted a couple of extended sessions which in many ways were one on one reruns of my wellbeing workshop. It was very important that Mike could work out the Human Given's ideas himself. He was particularly taken by my Pagoda Needs formulation (see my Feelbetter website) – which made a lot of sense to him and which he could clearly relate to his life now and indeed to his corporate life also.

He began to be much better after this and in a follow up session three months later, he was completely recovered. Not only was he actively enjoying his retirement with his wife and family and his many developing interests but he was also dealing in a completely different way with the inevitable tribulations of his week by week life.

e) Barbara and Ros – attempting to reset in mid-stream

I have talked of Mike, who in his retirement had to make certain changes to how he understood himself and so how he could better build a life that worked. He had time to do that and he had a strong story of a broadly successful working and family life to call on.

But what if you have reached a stage earlier than that,

say in your late forties, when you realise that something big has to change? That was the case for Barbara and Ros (not their real names). Both lived on their own and found themselves lonely and unfulfilled. Moreover, in dealing with this (or more accurately, failing to deal with this) they suffered chronically from depression which from time to time flared up into something much worse. This was the case for both of them, when they first came to me towards the end of 2013. Both were mentally exhausted and over dreaming and both were at their very limits.

Their situations on the face of it had different origins. For Ros, it was a very aggressive suspiciousness – of risking letting anybody in close. This was in fact a very understandable way to have handled her life as a teenager and young woman in her twenties – as she had through that time been "betrayed" by her father who left home suddenly and then when she herself left home, by very difficult relationships with men, including being raped and physically abused. She still used sex as a means of dealing with relationships and was quite promiscuous but her subsequent experiences then only served to confirm her in her view that she could not trust anybody. And her lack of trust extended to women as well and despite having a good career as a legal secretary was very much alone at work too.

For Barbara, the loneliness was much more obviously linked to a chronic lack of confidence, which in turn had been fuelled by unfortunate circumstances that meant that she could never establish herself. She had a history of failure at school and lacking parental support never found what she greatly needed from her teachers. She knew she was bright and could be very creative as a writer, but her potential was never realised. In fact it was worse than that – her life had become one of lowered expectations, both regarding the work she did and her chronic caution and fearfulness.

For both Ros and Barbara, their first desperate need was to find a way to be calmer – and by listening regularly to my Depression Mp3 and understanding the role over dreaming and rumination in feeding their depression, both were significantly improved at their second session.

But thereafter, their progress diverged. While Ros continued to make real improvement, I'm afraid that Barbara remained stuck and rather lost. My feeling was that this reflected Ros's much stronger resources compared to Barbara. Significantly Ros did have experiences of success and achievement in work and even relationships and as trance work cleared some of her older memories, she could begin to change how she saw her life possibilities. By contrast, Barbara's lacked these and so it was very hard to either find or enhance resources. It was very sad and unfortunate as there seemed no way that Barbara could sustain her improvement as she could not find the means and capacity to make the changes that she yearned for – to find creative endeavours and share these in some meaningful way.

f) Harold and his diagnosis of Dysthymia

It was only at the end of our first session that Harold revealed the shocking truth. That he was not depressed – no he had a diagnosis of Dysthymia. It had been made by a real expert on mental illness, namely his NHS psychiatrist and so this diagnosis must be treated with real respect. As a small detail and despite feeling pretty bad for months and having spent time seeing in addition, an NHS psychologist and a CBT therapist, Harold was still feeling just as rotten. Surprising I know as he had been under the care of real mental illness experts! He had been taking medication for a number of months (of course) but this had not helped (now there's a surprise) and he was ready to quit. So what is Dysthymia? I googled it and what I found was that it was the name given to an extended period of low mood – not depression you understand but a low mood, chronic and maybe quite mild at times.

Now it was true that at that first session I had found that Harold was not a good trance subject and he found it difficult to connect to emotionally stressful periods in his past. But Harold wanted to see me again and indeed came regularly for 10 sessions – which is a lot for me. In that first session and the next two we focussed on his work as a schools administrator which he found very unsatisfactory. He was also finding it very difficult to develop his career away from administration in ways he felt he wanted to, though in truth he showed no great enthusiasm for any change.

And then in our fourth session it began to emerge how difficult his marriage was and how hard he found it to create the life he felt he and his wife were looking for. So we spent 3 more sessions working on that. By this time, his wife had moved out (to find herself) and to his great surprise his mood began to lift. What was emerging was that their marriage was over and that this would be good for both of them. And quite quickly, pieces began to move into place for Harold. He met up with a couple of friends he had known for a long time and indeed there was another relationship, long on hold, which began to develop quite naturally. He also found he was enjoying his work rather more. And then Harold said that he felt he was ok and did not need to see me anymore. He also said at the end that he was not sure why exactly, but I had been the only therapist he had ever seen who he felt he got anything from and who he wanted to see again. And by the end he had junked both the psychologist and psychiatrist.

Looking back it seems pretty clear to me what was going on. It was Harold's marriage which just could not be made to work and the feelings he had around that – many of them quite disempowering. In other words he was stuck. I would say that that would be enough to lower anybody's mood and makes so much more sense than a pointless and meaningless label, however exalted was the person who chose it.

g) Fiona's recovery from Depression and a family campaign of ignorance and stigma

Fiona hails from the depths of Essex (the beautiful unspoiled part of it to the north, well away from the Thames) and came to see me very depressed and cowed by family pressures, not just from her husband but from her wider family (mainly siblings). She was in her early fifties with two girls approaching university age and had suffered from years of mainly verbal abuse and humiliation from her husband, a successful businessman.

As Fiona found herself sinking beneath the weight of this, she found that her wider family refused to believe that her husband could possibly be as she described it. They instinctively took his side and dismissed her concerns as reflecting badly on her – she was an attention seeker, delusional, going mad. Fiona believed that she could understand why her wider family were not open to listening to her – it went way back to her relationship with her siblings as children and young adults.

Nevertheless the consequences were devastating for her now and had been (she realised) for a number of years – sapping her self-confidence, forcing her to introspect and worry even more and making it much harder still for her to keep hold of who she was and what you knew she was capable of.

Fiona did need someone who could listen to her and take her side and inch her towards more empowering explanations of where she found herself. But more than that, she needed to take urgent action to gain some control of her rumination so that she would be able to dream a little less intensely and so find more energy and belief to deal with her situation. Fiona was an excellent trance subject and so in successive sessions spread over six weeks, I found that I could ease the trauma of her recent years, build her self-confidence by reminding her of all that she had achieved (at one time she had built a successful catering business) and help her to see what she could do to change her situation. It was clear that she did indeed need to leave her husband but she was determined to do this only when she was sure that her children would not suffer at this delicate stage in their lives.

By the time we finished, Fiona was much better. She was sleeping well and waking up refreshed. She was feeling much less vulnerable and resentful of her wider family and was much busier and occupied with friends and a new project. Finally, she felt herself much stronger in relation to her husband and was certain that she was not mad and knew where she was going.

h) How often do NHS psychiatrists get it as badly wrong as this?

I will have to watch myself here as I would hate to be accused of exhibiting dismissive superiority to my betters. Because Norman's experience with me (not his real name) was one of such rapid transformation that it would be hard not to question the NHS psychiatrists under whose care Norman was and not to wonder what the hell they are about and who the hell are they kidding.

Norman was in the early twenties who came to see me, seriously depressed, on heavy antidepressant medication, exhibiting classic OCD checking behaviours and under the outpatient care of a NHS psychiatrist. At his first session Norman scored 30 on the CORE system I use which is severe distress. He was sleeping badly and in particular waking up exhausted. He was spending far too much time on his own and really struggling at work (in media marketing).

He also said that he had been under a number of NHS psychiatrists over the years and none had helped him or he liked particularly or had any respect for, though the latest was "decent enough".

At our second session, Norman's CORE score had fallen to 19 and by the third session he was scoring just 4, an indicator of robust emotional health. And six weeks after that session he came around again as a check-up – and he was flying.

How did I help Norman so quickly? It was not rocket science.

At that first session, it quickly became evident that Norman had a clear and vivid access to memories that were still strongly arousing him. These concerned his early lonely and excluded experiences at his secondary school and later relationship experiences that had gone wrong. I explained the situation to Norman as follows: that strong and uncontrolled emotions, arising as a trauma like memory outside of his conscious control had been a constant feature of his life for many years and that his ways of coping with this had made matters worse. He had evolved OCD behaviours as an attempt to be more in control. Additionally his self confidence in group situations had been drained away and this led to excessive worrying and exhausting over dreaming, which he also sought to control by OCD checking behaviours.

To my surprise, Norman was a good trance subject which is often not the case for those on significant medication. And as his memories were so strong, it was clear that they could be detraumatised quite easily. And this was done in that first session using the Rewind method.

The effect was to calm Norman and allow him to begin to regain control of his emotions. And then what happened for Norman was what could be confidently anticipated. Namely that his self-confidence would grow, especially in social situations and his OCD behaviours, already weakening would disappear completely.

I wrote a letter to his NHS psychiatrist after Norman saw him for the last time – curious to see if he might acknowledge his incapacity to help Norman and maybe be interested in how I had helped Norman. And did he? What do you think?

i) How Depression can creep up quietly – but then can be dealt with

Sometimes depression creeps up unnoticed and then just hangs around, like stale cigarette smoke. It is only when you stop to notice or something changes in your life that pulls you up, that you are reminded of how unsatisfactory life is and how chronically rotten you have been feeling. This was the case for Donald (not his real name).

Donald was a Scot in his mid-forties who had been living down south for most of his adult life. He was happily married with two daughters. He worked for himself as an IT consultant on mainly public sector projects – where his expertise and contacts were. His elder daughter had suffered from chronic health problems that were a persistent source of worry. Donald himself was also not in the best of health as he suffered from allergies. Finally business was tougher now, as the cuts were biting.

Donald found it hard to relax, was always worrying

about something, was sleeping badly and according to the CORE measure, was moderately distressed. He told me that he had been that way for years. He talked of a happy childhood on the east coast of Scotland and there was nothing in his background that was obviously causing him difficulties. No it was his life now.

In helping Donald, I began my reviewing much of the main Human Givens insights – of being able to take action to get needs met for emotional wellbeing and the importance of getting emotional arousal levels down. This made a lot of sense to Donald as he could begin to see his situation in a more empowering way. We practised 7/11 breathing and on two successive sessions of therapy, I used deep trance to remind Donald of his strength and capacities and the gifts of his life. Finally, it was necessary to help Donald rebalance his life a little and moderate his emotional attachment to his work – again trance was helpful here.

By the end of our work together, Donald was much more relaxed, sleeping better and self-evidently dreaming less.

j) Carol's remarkable story – at last fighting free from a lifetime of depression

Carol has been seeing me on and off now for almost four years. This is her story – of an adult life time of depression and how she is now over it, at least most of the time but not yet confidently so. She is happy for me to share her story and so what follows is my understanding of it (with just a few small details changed including her name, and a couple of big things omitted for reasons of privacy and respect).

Carol is now in her mid-fifties and when she first found me had been depressed since her early twenties. And she really had – at times to the point of extinction and total exhaustion but even when the pressure lifted through these years, the depression never really went away. When she came to me, she was on heavy antidepressant medication and knew that she needed it.

Carol would say that she has now been free of her depression for eighteen months. In fact she now knows that she is not her depression: it was just something that happened to her. She is now taking only a small dosage of anti-depressants and even when she fears that her depression might be coming back, she wants to contend with that, without increasing her dosage.

Carol is one of the most remarkable, resourceful and determined people I have ever come across (though she would hate me to say that). And yes, there were issues in her past that needed to be resolved and cleared. One of these related to her relationship to her father, which came to the fore at the time of his death. Another was a very private experience in her early twenties, which she could only face and deal with now, essentially by at last being emotionally strong enough to acknowledge her culpability and loss around it.

So why did the depression stay for so long and is now gone and why is Carol so remarkable and resourceful? These questions are two sides of the same coin.

Carol was depressed for so long because she has had to

contend with so much just going wrong for her – relating to her essential human needs of work, financial security and intimacy. That despite her best efforts, these life difficulties persisted. She was a single mother, bringing up two children (who were now young adults). And she was a teacher and never quite realised just how much she hated what she did – not the teaching mainly but everything else that surrounded it. It was only when she realised that she had to do something else – when she finally understood just how much she hated teaching that her depression began to ease. And now as I write this, her shoulder is injured and she cannot dance, which she loves.

But that she kept going, resourcefully looking for what she needed to do and to change to get her life back on track. How remarkable is that?

But she never knew why her life problems were affecting her so much. She never understood how excessive rumination causes exhausting over dreaming. But now she does.

She is training in law and working in paralegal jobs such that she can use her talents for hard work and graft. So she knows how to keep clear of depression, to be thinking and acting better and to keep going. Carol just needs her luck to change. She deserves that.

k) Clear Trauma and Depression can just melt away – the experience of two women

Here is a brief outline of the amazingly quick recovery from serious depression of two clients. I will call them

Padma and Roberta (not their real names).

Padma had been born in the UK, her parents having emigrated from India. She had three growing up children and worked part time to supplement the family budget. Roberta was a single Mum with a teenage son, in a new relationship and needing to work full time in a demanding job in the hotel industry.

Both were in their forties and very capable. And against all that they could ever have expected, were lost in a classic depression. Both were over dreaming and consequently waking up exhausted. The result was a downward spiral fuelled by unproductive worrying and introspection and excessive and exhausting REM dreaming sleep.

Moreover it was continuing to unravel for them as their family responsibilities and duties were harder and harder to discharge. They had no idea what was going on and neither had their GP (of course) – who could only offer anti-depressants and/or an appointment (months into the future) for CBT. But they could not wait for the latter (though of course not knowing just how unsatisfactory CBT would probably be) and were reluctant to embark on the former (and for good reason).

For both Padma and Roberta, it did not take long to discover that each was still traumatised by the death of their mother, respectively some three and ten years previously. For them to go back to the experience reignited high arousal and emotional memories and when they thought about it, they both said that they "had not been right" since.

I burned my overcoming depression Mp3 for both to listen to (so they could understand why the depression was taking hold) and in the second session, I used the Rewind technique to clear the emotion around these memories. Rewind is an effective non-voyeuristic trance method to de-traumatise strong past memories from the limbic system.

Both were very resourceful women and with the trauma cleared and then the over dreaming, worrying and depression lifting, they found they could deal with their other life difficulties. Within next to no time, a virtuous circle of control, hope and lowering arousal replaced the previous vicious circle. For both, the depression was gone in less than a month and that it would stay gone, I had little doubt.

l) Peeling away the layers of an onion – how Tricia recovered from depression

Sometimes, people have been depressed for so long – not necessarily all the time but chronically – that they have accepted the depression as central to who they are and the life that they lead. They don't believe in their heart that they will ever escape completely from the depression. They have tried anti-depressants or indeed may still be taking them (and scared to stop even though they don't seem to be doing much good). This was true of Tricia. (Tricia is not her real name and other details below have also been changed.)

Tricia was in her mid-sixties, married and with three grown up children and now five grandchildren. She traced the beginning of her depression to a time some twenty five years previously. This was a time of great stress when her mother had died, she had been made redundant and there were money worries to contend with. At times over these past twenty five years, it had got so bad that she was considered a suicide risk and had spent time in hospital, heavily medicated.

Tricia was quite naturally resistant to the idea that her depression could be simply explained – by ruminating too much and so slipping into a vicious circle of over dreaming and exhaustion. She also found after our first session, that my Overcoming Depression Mp3, though "interesting" had clearly not got through to her. She was though a very good trance subject (as many depressed clients are) and so in addition to some very gentle guided imagery, I used the Rewind in that second session to detraumatise the memories around her crisis of twenty five years ago.

At our next session, the emotion around those memories of that time had clearly faded but she was still feeling stressed and depressed – scoring a little better on the CORE system I use, but not that much better. So we went further back to her childhood where we discovered patterns of insecurity related to living just with her mother and severe money worries. We also spent time looking at her relationship with her children and how she could be different with them and so enjoy her grandchildren much more. Finally we discussed her day to day life now and how she could do certain things differently and find small pleasures.

It was like peeling away the layers of an onion – until

all that was left was Tricia as she actually always could have been – capable, efficient and busy and at last clear to live a life that would work for her. And four months later, her depression has still gone.

m) When fear of depression is the problem – Trevor's experience

I was learning Human Givens, had not yet completed my practical training but was managing to find people to work with, from all kinds of places – from friends, a depression help group, a very helpful nutritionist with lots of clients in emotional difficulty and so on. Yet I still remember clearly (this is going back ten years) a man in his forties coming to me who was almost permanently locked in depression. Or to put it more accurately – he was never ever free from it and every so often and for no good reason, he fell back into a black despairing hole.

I remember that he could recall vividly his first depression. It was while he was at secondary school and if memory serves me (going back all these years) it had a lot to do with bullying and being unable to complete his exams. I could be wrong about the detail of it. But what was so clear was how terrifying and immediate that depression memory was for him – even after 25 years or more. And so I detraumatised that memory – using the Rewind technique. All Human Givens therapists are taught Rewind and it works so well for so many. But this was about my first time using it in a serious therapy situation. And it "worked".

Therapy was very new and fresh for me then and I had

not built up a memory and experience bank of successful help and of course interventions that were less successful. But I remember how transformational the rewind was for that man. He never looked back after that session.

And since then, I have always been aware if my depressed clients are living with a great traumatic fear of their first depression. That in consequence, they are always on high alert looking for signs of the depression returning. And so, unfortunately and tragically they find themselves locked in chronic and what seems like, permanent depression or near depression.

I would say that perhaps one in four of my depressed clients need to have an original depression experience detraumatised and for maybe a half of these, that is all that they need.

And that has been true of a recent client – whom I will call Trevor. He was also in his mid-forties and with a wife, young child, a job as a floorer and doing GSCE evening classes in maths and science (having left school with nothing) – was on the face of it living a life that was working pretty well. Trevor had had an eventful earlier life with drugs, alcohol and criminality very much part of it. But he had escaped this and seemed clear of it. But what was still active was the memory of a terrible depression just as he was freeing himself from this part of his life. I did wonder whether part of the fear was of the memories of his earlier life and the terror of falling back into it. No matter, we detraumatised his memories around all of this using the Rewind technique, and he is now free from his serial depressions and of the fear of falling back into them.

I wonder how many depressed people today are still terrified of their first depression experience? For these, the memory must be cleared before permanent recovery can take place? But this can be done.

CHAPTER 26

BE A DEPRESSION RECOVERY OPTIMIST

Depression is not a mystery to understand and neither should it be something to be scared of. But, there is so little understanding of what a depression is and this leaves a lot of space for real rubbish to be written. This in turn explains why depression can be held in such awe. It reflects how little it is understood – allied to the recognition of the terrible suffering a seriously depressed individual can endure. And if you see this in others or endure it yourself and not know what is going on and have the dawning realisation that neither do the experts, why then naturally you will be scared.

This is how a depression takes hold – according to the Human Givens approach and as I have understood it from the many that have come to me seriously depressed and out of hope? It is all about useless worrying as depression is a brain that is absolutely exhausted, by worrying incessantly and without any result or resolution.

1. Something happens in your life that pushes you off balance... and you quite naturally and healthily begin to worry about it, looking for a solution that will calm you and bring you back to equilibrium.

2. But this does not happen and as the problem persists, it becomes harder and harder to deal with. And you are aware of those rigid thinking habits that arise whenever you are under pressure and maybe also the emotion of bad past memories - and as these impose themselves, it is even more

difficult to get your life back on track.

3. Then you're sleeping begins to deteriorate and in particular you are increasingly tired and exhausted in the morning when you wake up. You may also be dimly aware that you are dreaming much more.

At this stage, a downward spiral really gets underway - the classic signs of depression.

4. Your problems then become harder and harder to deal with and seem to be multiplying and as motivation and energy disappear, you worry more and more, introspecting and blaming yourself.

What is happening is you are locking into a depression trance, focussing internally and negatively, losing hope and as good deep wave sleep becomes pushed out by excessive dreaming, you may finally be finding that physical aches and pains add to your sense of hopelessness and stuckness - another of the signs of depression.

This used to be called a state of nervous exhaustion and you can see why. If very severe, this can even transmute into psychotic experiences.

Depression – a simple summary

Depression is the mental and physical exhaustion caused by the body's need to dream more than it is capable of, in order to deal with a situation that appears increasingly impossible.

And why is there the need to engage in high energy dreaming? It is the attempt to clear the excessive levels of arousal, worrying and exhaustion, which caused the problem in the first place.

And so we have a vicious circle where symptoms and signs of depression multiply

And what feeds the depression vicious circle?

1. This will relate to the difficulty of your life situation now and the nature and extent of the crisis that might have triggered your depression and have stopped you living a life that works?

2. Then there are your resources – how well are your emotions, habitual patterns of thinking and responding helping or not to get your essential needs met?

3. Finally, it is important to discover if there is trauma lurking somewhere in your past as often it is the active reliving of past traumas that is the main inhibitor to one's capacity to get a life working better.

Many describe Depression as being locked in their worrying brain, unable to escape from useless and obsessive rumination, often of a "what is wrong with me" nature - a terrifying trance state of inward obsession. To be depressed is an added layer of misery often piled upon genuine challenges, further reducing the person's ability to cope with their difficulties

Hope is the one thing that all Depressed people lack?

This lack is the hope that there is a way back to emotional health and that this way back is one that can be embarked on quickly and easily - that there is a clear light shining at the end of the tunnel.

And why is the restoration of hope so vital? It is because those lost in depression will typically have little or no hope of recovery and what hope they have will be fast ebbing away – that their efforts to deal with the depression have defeated them. What I find amongst all of the depressed clients that I help is resignation, defeat and hopelessness. And this is why I know that what they need right away, beginning in that first session is the seed of some hope.

Of course, if you are lost in depression, you cannot easily be fooled. You have good reason and bitter experience to support your hopelessness – that whatever you try does not work and whoever you ask for help and understanding fails so abysmally. And so those who do speak with little authority (even the experts) will be seen through. Which adds to the hopelessness?

"Where can I find what I need?" … and "does it exist?" are questions that the depressed will be screaming inside.

But hope is there waiting. All that is needed is to look in the right place. A simple explanation that will make complete sense of why you are feeling as you do, and then guidance with the first steps that can be taken right away.

And then guess what? Hope stirs.

And if you want to get moving towards hope right now then listen to my ***35 minute Lift Depression Mp3***. And you will see what begins to bring back hope is an understanding of what is happening to you and why and the beginning of action that you can take that will get you moving.

It is hard for to me to overstate the importance of this - that depression is not a mystery and neither is it very complicated. And you certainly don't need a postgraduate degree in psychiatry to have any hope of understanding it.

That is one reason why I ask my clients to listen to my depression MP3 and why I may ask that they read chunks of my Feelbetter Counselling and Depression Recovery websites - what depression is, symptoms and diagnosis, and case studies, profiles and testimonials and of course my two depression blogs. And why this book has been written.

Have you come across Hebbian learning? This is that to learn something, you need to be exposed to what you wish to learn many times and in many different ways - such that it really stinks in. It is not enough to hear something once or to read something just once and expect it to stick. No, we need to be exposed to the same ideas in different ways in different formats — reading, hearing and direct experiencing. And then in time it will stay and you will really know it. This is what I am trying to do with depression — so you really get it.

You are not gone mad, there is a credible explanation of why you're feeling as you are and there is a route out for you.. If you really understand why this is so, then lo and behold you should find that hope will return – and this will be genuine, rooted and real.

What do I do when Hope just will not revive?

The cultivation and restoration of hope is essential for depression recovery as the absence of hope is the common experience of pretty well every depressed client that I have ever seen.

And there is no doubt that in helping my clients take that first hopeful step to recovery, it is so exciting (for both of us) to feel the warm glow of hope begin to return. As I have suggested, hope can best be kindled by a clear understanding of what a depression is – and for the large majority of my depressed clients, this is enough for this first step on the road to recovery. The contrast between the elegant simplicity and credibility of the Human Givens explanation of depression (that it is a REM sleep disorder fuelled by rumination out of control) and the mishmash, confusion and sheer vacuity of the conventional depression explanation is stark indeed – as between Shakespeare and Mr Men perhaps or Beethoven and Britain's Got Talent.

But what of the depressed clients I see who do not respond to such explanations? What to do then?

The answer is that it all depends – on why this explanation fails to take root. And there are broadly, three reasons.

The first is that it can be that my client is so lost and ground down by their failure and desperation to create a life that works, that my words of explanation just cannot penetrate. Second and separately, there are depressed individuals who have worked so hard and resourcefully to find the answer to their depression over many years that now they are literally giving up. There have been so many false hope trails laid, that one more just cannot do it for them anymore. And what is the third reason? It is that there is some powerful traumatic memory that remains ever present snd so drowns out everything else.

If there is trauma, then the essential immediate requirement is to clear it. And thankfully, this can be done in the large majority of cases using the trance methods taught to all Human Givens practitioners. And if this does indeed lift the trauma then that alone will be a massive demonstration that change is possible and hope will then flood in.

But for those who are ground down and unable to accept that change is possible, the only answer I know is to take it more gently - but knowing that somehow or other, a spark of hope must be kindled.

Sometimes a direct experience of deep trance relaxation can be sufficiently unexpected and surprising to be enough to open these clients to the possibility of change. And, sometimes hope can begin by moving immediately to the second thread of my depression recovery programme - which is firefighting action to get rumination down. I'll be covering this below.

And there will be times when somehow or other, a key can be found that will unlock and open the door just sufficiently to let hope in from the cold. That there is a word or reframe that challenges something sufficiently that there is some movement for my client - and with this movement comes the possibility of change and with that of course there will be hope also.

My three threads for Depression recovery – is it down to me?

I have been talking at length about the essential importance of building hope for those suffering from depression. I see hope as the first of the three threads that need to be weaved together into a fabric that can support genuine and lasting depression recovery. The other two threads are fire fighting to get rumination down and a partnership between me and my client to repair resources and get their life working much better.

So there you have it, Hope, Firefighting and Partnership - my three threads for depression recovery. I am saying that these three threads can be woven together into a garment that will be sufficiently warm and strong that most of my depressed clients will not only recover from their depression but will stay free of it.

But am I saying that these three threads can be followed by anybody to bring about depression recovery? Or am I only revealing how I work as a depression recovery therapist?

The truth is that it may be closer to the latter. There is an industry of self-help books and advice on all subjects under the sun including depression relief. This is not what I am about. I'm not saying follow these three steps and you will get over your depression or if you are a therapist, all you have to do is to follow these steps and you too will become an effective depression recovery therapist. No, I am saying is that this is how I see it for the depressed clients who come to me.

Yes I do hope that a lot of what I'm saying will be helpful and interesting and that my proven success as a therapist gives me the authority to be heard. But I am only talking about what I do.

You will already have read that in the field of counselling psychotherapy, it is not the model of therapy that counts but the quality of the therapist. So how can I ever confidently say that what I do and how I do it will work for everybody?

And this means finally that however hard I try to be clear and transparent about how I work, something always will be unexplained and inexplicable. And that goes to the heart of the mystery of what it is that distinguishes successful therapists from those who sadly are not nearly as good.

There is no doubt that part of what I am trying to do as a therapist (and by writing this book and the interviews that support this book) is to project my authority and so invite my clients to put their faith in me and to trust me. And when kindling hope for my client, it is my authority that is on the line.

Firefighting – the second thread

If you're weaving a blanket and using just three threads, then each of these threads will have a very important role in creating the blanket's colour, texture and design. Yes, each thread might be introduced at a different stage but before very long all three will be involved to create the vision of the blanket designer. There are three threads in my depression recovery programme and these are Hope, Firefighting and Partnership. And having shown where Hope fits in, let's talk about Firefighting.

Firefighting is quite clearly distinct from Hope and in logic should follow on from the first requirement to kindle Hope. But there is little doubt also that as Firefighting proceeds, this will nurture Hope and may even jumpstart it.

What do I mean by Firefighting? It is the urgent immediate action needed to reduce rumination and so allow sleep to become more restful and replenishing. This will happen as the need to dream subsides. If you remember, it is overwhelming and useless rumination that requires a large amount of exhausting REM dreaming sleep to discharge and neutralise the rumination and this feeds and maintains depression. So if rumination can be reduced then surprisingly quickly (and probably within just a few days) sleep will become more refreshing. This will be good for the generation of Hope of course and will lead naturally into action and movement that can begin to get a life that works much better.

The key to Firefighting is distraction. It is about

distracting attention and filling up one's mind in activity that shifts you away from useless rumination – which is a trance state of inward self-obsession. My inclination is to leave this as much as possible to my client but to make suggestions of course. There may be clearing up and tidying up work to be done at home, there may be visits to be made to friends or family that haven't been seen for a long time and perhaps there are some treats and surprises that you could plan for yourself that would take you out of your normal self-obsessed routine. And with a perspective that understands the short-term benefit of successful Firefighting, visits to the gym and the planning and cooking of nutritious food can play a part. Firefighting is about doing small things a little differently and noticing the change and the more refreshing sleep that follows on very quickly.

And if the Firefighting stage begins to yield results such that energy and motivation begin to return then there is a natural linkage into the third thread, which I call Partnership.

Partnership – the third thread

The aim of the partnership between my client and me is easy to say. It is that my client is better living a life that works – where my client's resources are working effectively so that he or she is getting her essential emotional needs pretty well met – not necessarily perfectly but balanced nicely between them.

I have expressed this in terms of the Human Givens organising idea because this makes so much sense and because it means that the focus is on action and change in the way a life is led rather than focusing entirely on pathology. Clearly if someone is living a life that is working then they are most unlikely to be depressed (any disagreement there?) while most depressions begin with a life that is neither working nor can be made to work. Actually it is often more than that – that the depression damages the not working well life such that it is working even less well.

So how do I go about my side of the partnership?

All efforts must be directed in just two directions. First, to get arousal levels down so that sleep improves and second to help the client problem solve so that they can take the action needed to get their life working better. And this in turn may require the healing of emotional resources caused by past trauma and strong emotional patterning

These two directions are obviously closely connected. The high arousal of a depressed person is a trancelike self-obsessed focus, which destroys the capacity to problem solve and so correct the underlying lack that caused the depression in the first place. And the mere fact of being able to problem solve and so take control gives a sense of hope and movement and is therefore a highly effective way to reduce arousal.

First I listen and watch carefully to understand how and in what direction my client would wish to move in and then to relate this is best I can to the needs formulation is understood by Human Givens. This is normally quite easy to do as HG needs makes so much sense and is intuitively understood by everyone. Often the needs gap relates to relationships or to work. This could be close one-on-one relationships or more distant family and group relationships. In terms of work they can be understood in terms both of career or family or indeed more in terms of hobbies and wider understandings of what brings meaning and purpose.

The other area where needs are never met for someone enduring depression is in the area of control - notably control of emotions. Indeed it is the lack of control of emotions and being able to use them rather than having them overruling and overriding that creates the fear and worry that drives the depression in the first place. And of course in order to live a life that works, the most important resource most of us have is how our emotions are working. (See chapter 22).

In summary, I see my task in the partnership as helping to heal emotional resources so that there is greater control and capacity to get a life that is working (to get essential emotional needs better met). Yes it is important to set meaningful goals and it is equally important to begin a process that opens to beneficial movement and change. This means beginning to reverse the vicious circle into a virtuous circle.

How do I do this? Look at chapters 22 and 23 about what makes good counselling and understanding the Human Givens to get a better idea.

And to see how the three threads fit together in practice, look at these seven summary points – my experience in helping depressed clients.

I will typically use the following to facilitate healing

1. Explaining what depression is so that my client does not feel that they are to blame. This often leads to 'light bulb' moments which are in themselves liberating and relaxing

2. Undertake a Needs audit so that the client can begin to perceive their situation differently and in a more empowering way and so can begin to see how they can begin to shift. As part of this I may very well make suggestions and recommend tasks that that lead to understanding of the changes that might be needed and the options that are available. All of this is designed to reduce arousal and to engage the client's problem-solving capacity.

3. Investigate whether there is trauma or threshold trauma that is prompting high arousal. And if there is, then to clear this trauma which all Human Givens practitioners are trained to do, using trance methods.

4. Take every opportunity from the beginning to reframe - which may be directed at softening strong black-and-white thinking or suggesting more empowering explanations of the past.

5. Explicit trance work - designed to impart an experience of relaxation, to access the client's strengths and resources, to heal habits and emotional patterns that are not helpful and to rehearse beneficial changes.

6. To complement this, I will also encourage or even insist that my client listens regularly (daily) to my Lift Depression Mp3.

7. But one thing that I will not do, at least not until my client is beginning to feel better - is to allow any extended talk that focuses on the past and all the bad that seems to be there and their theories of why they are feeling so bad. Indeed at that first session I tend to do more of the talking, which often is a great relief for my client.

ABOUT THE AUTHOR

For thirty years Andrew worked as a professional economist; in Africa (Swaziland) and for the UK Treasury, then in the city and finally as a consultant financial economist. He was born in 1948.

He began his journey to his counselling practice at the beginning of the century. During this time, he studied and meditated extensively, particularly following Buddhist practice and studied the Enneagram personality typing system. This culminated in intensive Human Givens training in 2001-2004.

He has been practicing full time since 2005 from his home in South Woodford, East London. He lives with his second wife and young daughter.

Andrew has been suffering from a chronic and slowly progressing MS (multiple sclerosis) for many years. It has reached the stage where walking is tricky. Yet despite this his capacity to practice his therapy at home is not in any way compromised. And the wellbeing lessons he shares with his clients are for him as well.

His online presence includes

Printed in Great Britain
by Amazon